About the Author

Marianne Rogerson has worked in the Scottish events industry for the past seven years. Now a Director of party planning business FizzPizzazz (www.fizzpizzazz.co.uk) and a Director of honeymoon wedding list company HoneyMoney (www.honeymoney.co.uk), she has come a long way since running the Cocktail Society at Edinburgh University! Ever the multi-tasker, she wrote *Your Scottish Wedding* whilst planning her own wedding at Dundas Castle in December 2004.

About the Photographer

Having won her first photographic competition at the age of 12, Sarah Hutson (www.sarahelizabeth.co.uk) has gone on to win the title of both Scotland's Most Promising Wedding and Portrait Photographer in 2001 and more recently the titles of Scotland's Avant Garde Wedding Photographer of the year in 2002 and 2003. She is qualified to an associate level in Master Photographers Association and started her own company, Sarah Elizabeth Photography, in 2003.

Order of Service

◇ ◇ ◇

Processional Music
ST. ANTHONY CHORALE ... ... Attributed to Haydn

FIRST HYMN

As the deer pants for the water,
So my soul longs after You.
You alone are my heart's desire
And I long to worship You.

Refrain
You alone are my strength, my shield,
To You alone may my spirit yield.
You alone are my heart's desire
And I long to worship You.

I want You more than gold or silver,
Only You can satisfy.
You alone are the real joy-giver
And the apple of my eye.

You alone are my strength, my shield,
To You alone may my spirit yield.
You alone are my heart's desire
And I long to worship You.

You're my Friend and You're my Brother,
Even though you are a King.
I love You more than any other,
So much more than anything.

You alone are my strength, my shield,
To You alone may my spirit yield.
You alone are my heart's desire
And I long to worship You.

THE MARRIAGE

Your
Scottish Wedding

A Modern Bride's Guide to
Planning her Big Day

MARIANNE ROGERSON

Luath Press Limited
EDINBURGH

www.luath.co.uk

First published 2006

The paper used in this book is recyclable. It is made from
low chlorine pulps produced in a low-energy, low emission manner
from renewable forests.

Photographs © Sarah Hutson

Printed by Scotprint, Haddington

Typeset in 10pt Sabon and Frutiger

Contents

CONTENTS

Page 11:   First things first!
            Choosing your date
            Bringing in the professionals
            Your dream team
            Best Man
            Maid of Honour and Bridesmaids
            Flower girls / Page boys
            Ushers
            Father of the bride
            Mother of the bride
            Other roles
            Who does what?
            How much?
            Who pays for what?
            Organising your finances

Page 25:   Making it legal
            Who can be married in Scotland?
            Types of marriage
            Civil partnerships
            How and when to give notice
            If you live in England or Wales
            Documents to be produced
            If you are domiciled outside the United Kingdom
            Making arrangements for the marriage ceremony
            The marriage schedule
            Marriage certificate

Contents

Page 33: Location! Location! Location!
Licence
Numbers
Location and accommodation
Cost
Calculating your venue cost
Narrowing down your search
Questions to ask... the venue
What's your style?

Page 45: I do!
Civil or Religious?
Finding a Minister/Priest/Registrar
Music
Prelude
Entrance
Some of the more popular entrance tunes
Hymns
Some of the more popular wedding hymns
Signing the marriage schedule
The processional/retiral music

Page 55: Who wears what and how
THE BRIDE
The dress
The shopping trip
How it works
Hiring
Having it designed
Something more traditional?
Surprise!
Money wise!
Looking after your dress
Accessories

Contents

Something old, something new, something borrowed,
    something blue
Bridesmaids
Where to shop
The Groom and Groomsmen

Page 75:   Do it *your* way
Personalising your day
Theming ideas
You are cordially invited...
Invitations
What else should be included in the envelope?
Example A–Z
Orders of service
Flower power
Have your cake and eat it
Do me a favour!
Party time!

Page 101:   Picture perfect
Which style?
Choosing your photographer
Questions to ask... your shortlisted photographers
Putting together your shot list
Videography

Page 111:   Get me to the church on time
What's your style?
Horse and carriage
Vintage car
Stretch limo
Supercar
Something more unusual?
Car etiquette
Guests

CONTENTS

Contents

Page 117:   Eat Drink and be merry
            Choosing your caterer
            Questions to ask... your caterer
            Order of the day
            Drinks reception
            Receiving line
            Thanking the piper
            Wedding breakfast
            Factors to consider when planning your wedding breakfast
            Your menu
            Top tips for choosing your wine
            Seating plan
            Top table
            Guests
            Numbered or named?
            Speeches
            Order of speeches and toasts
            Additional speeches
            Entertainment
            First dance
            Something a bit different
            Don't forget the children
            Mingling with your guests

Page 137:   Hey, good looking!
            Lifestyle
            Diet
            Skin
            Hair
            Nails
            Make-up

Contents

Page 145: It's a wrap!
           Gift list etiquette
           Present showing
           The choice is yours
           The Internet
           Things to consider

Page 151: Girls behaving badly!
           Who does what?
           Feet Washing
           What's your style?
           Hen nights with a difference
           The Blackening
           Get away!
           Tips for the organiser

Page 159: Get Away!
           Beach bliss
           Multi-destination holidays
           Activity and adventure
           Go it alone
           A European jaunt
           On the doorstep
           Timing is everything!

Page 167: On the ball
           The bridal countdown
           Lists, lists, lists
           Managing your guest list
           Wedding file
           Wedding boxes
           Detailed schedule
           Looking ahead

Contents

Page 181:   Showtime!
            Wedding day plan
            The bride's emergency bag
            Bride's overnight bag
            When things go wrong

Page 191:   Your Scottish Wedding Directory

First things first!

So, you're engaged... congratulations!

Before you embark on the massive adventure that is planning your wedding, there are many things that you will need to get sorted before you go any further: Where? When? Who? How?
And ... how much?

First things first!

Choosing your date

You may have an idea of a possible date in your head – but you will need to decide how flexible you are prepared to be. Many sought after wedding venues get booked up years in advance, especially in the traditional wedding months. If you are adamant that you have to get married on a Saturday in August you may well have to wait two or three years for your desired venue to become available. Mid-week weddings in the out-of-season months may be more readily available and may well cost less, although it is worth remembering that this is less often the case with hotels, as less popular wedding dates are more popular corporate conference dates, which is where many hotels make the majority of their money.

When choosing your date, try to take into account other events which are likely to affect your guests. You may not care much for football, but if you plan your wedding for the same day as the World Cup Final, you may not have many male friends there! Think also of local events which may interrupt your proceedings, even if they don't directly involve your guests. Trying to organise your wedding day around the time of Hogmanay or the Edinburgh Festival, for example, will hugely affect your guests chances of finding reasonably priced flights and/or accommodation. I know of one bride who arranged her big day in London on the same day as the Gay Pride march – half her guests missed the ceremony because of the traffic problems caused. A bit of research at the beginning could save you a lot of grief in the long run.

The day of the week is also something to take into consideration. Friday weddings are becoming more popular as couples are organising weekend extravaganzas with additional celebrations continuing into the Saturday, but it does mean your guests taking a day off work. Equally, if your guests are travelling, a Sunday wedding may mean they have to take the Monday off (or worse still, it may affect their party spirit if they know they have to get up early for work the next day!)

First things first!

Time of year will have a huge impact on the type of wedding you have. The summer months of June to August continue to be the most popular months to get married in Scotland, as brides hope for a sunny day for their photographs, for drinks on the lawn and to be able to wear their strapless dresses and strappy shoes without hiding under an umbrella or having to worry about getting cold. A good summer day in Scotland, with the rhododendrons in full bloom and the warm weather, can form the perfect setting for a perfect wedding. However, remember this is Scotland and it is not renowned for its predictable weather! If you do plan to get married at this time of year, don't set your heart on having sunny, warm weather and if you are planning any part of the proceedings outdoors, make contingency plans for rain. Remember also that the midges come out in full force on summer evenings, which may not go down too well with the men in kilts!

Winter is becoming more and more popular – especially closer to Christmas time when theming opportunities abound – as brides become more enthusiastic about the possibility of a snow covered winter wonderland for their big day. Again, however, with the unpredictable Scottish weather, don't rely on anything. Take care also if you are planning your winter wedding in a remote location, particularly in the Highlands, as there is a distinct possibility of your guests not being able to make it due to bad weather conditions.

Off-season weddings can be a great option – summer months can become a bit wedding-tastic, and your guests may be thankful that yours is not the fifth in a row that they have to go to! Spring brings beautiful flower options, and the trees are certainly at their most stunning in autumn with the rich golds, reds and yellows – perfect for theming your big day around.

Bringing in the professionals

Many people think that hiring a professional wedding co-ordinator is a luxury they just cannot afford. However, with more brides these days working full-time and having a more available disposable income, the American trend for hired help is growing in the UK.

In some part of the USA, it is said the second phone call a girl makes when she gets engaged is to her wedding planner (after calling her parents)! Not only will a professional organiser save you valuable time and take the stress out of the whole planning process, they will also be able to help with ideas, recommend the best value and most reliable suppliers and help smooth out any problems that you come across... remember that they have been there and seen it all before! Very often too a wedding organiser will earn their money back for you – not only can they negotiate much better deals with suppliers than you would be able to, but they are used to working to budget and will not be tempted to overspend on every little detail like you will. (And believe me, you will!)

When choosing a wedding co-ordinator, even more importantly than any other wedding supplier, you need to find someone with whom you have a good rapport and who shares your vision for your wedding. Most wedding co-ordinators will offer a free consultancy so that you can establish whether you are going to work well together. They will then provide you with a costed report of what they will provide for you – remember that they don't have to be involved in the entire wedding. Perhaps you just require help with the entertainment, or the theming of the venue – and most co-ordinators provide an on-the-day co-ordinating service. Ensure that you understand the way in which the co-ordinator charges for their time – some will charge by the hour, others a percentage of the total services provided and some will charge a flat fee.

Your dream team

Choose your attendants wisely – not because you feel you ought to, or because someone is pressuring you to, but because they are people who are important to you and who you think will do a good job.

Being chosen to be a best man, bridesmaid or usher is a huge honour – but it can also be a huge responsibility. Think about what you will require of your attendants and choose people who you believe will be able and happy to perform these duties. Also, be sure to let them know upfront what you will expect from them.

First things first!

Understand too that if they feel the responsibility is too much they may decline your request – it's not something they have to do.

Some couples prefer to go it alone – but if you are considering being attendant-less, be realistic – on the morning of the wedding, you won't have time to check all the place cards are in place, the candles are lit, hand out the orders of service, make sure everyone gets on the right coach *and* look absolutely gorgeous! Having a good team behind you will make a huge difference to how smoothly the lead-up to and the day itself runs and some people may resent being pulled in to do all the work without the honour of being part of the bridal party.

It is a good idea to get all your attendants together before the wedding if possible, even if it is just for a drink after the rehearsal on the evening before the wedding. This gives you a chance to introduce anyone who doesn't already know each other and to make sure everyone knows who is responsible for what. Don't be embarrassed to give people written lists of their duties; they may be pleased to have something to refer to.

Best Man

Being chosen to be someone's best man can be a daunting experience – all those eyes on you, waiting for you to make them laugh during your speech! The groom's best friend may be the nicest man on Earth but if he can't speak in public or is a complete disaster when it comes to organising a night out, he's perhaps not best man material. However, there is more to being a best man than organising the stag night and making a speech – although those are possibly the most important roles these days. Your best man will need to be reliable and organised for a number of reasons (see 'Who does what?' box) and will also need to be able to keep the groom calm and organised in the lead-up to and on the wedding day.

Can't choose between friends? Don't worry; having two best men (perhaps a brother and a friend) is becoming more common, or why not have a best man and a groomsman? The groomsman could take the place of the Master of Ceremonies, allowing him to add to the speeches if he wishes. Another option is to have a best woman (normally the groom's sister) which is also becoming a more popular option these days – although if the stag night is strictly men only, this might not be a wise choice, unless the groom is happy to organise the stag night himself.

Maid of Honour and Bridesmaids

Bridesmaids traditionally dressed the same as the bride to confuse the evil spirits and protect the bride. Nowadays I assume you won't be too worried about evil spirits but it is still nice to have some good friends around you to share in both the lead-up to and the big day itself (and of course to organise your hen night!) Your bridesmaids will be a great support to you in the lead-up to your wedding. When you feel you have bored everyone else to tears with talk of your wedding, you can always call on your bridesmaids because – after all – they've agreed to be a part of it, haven't they?! It is also fun to have someone to share the excitement of dress and shoe shopping, and to discuss make-up and hair with. And, of course, on the morning of your wedding, getting all dressed up without a friend there to hand you a glass of champagne and get all teary-eyed as she puts your tiara in place wouldn't be half the fun!

Traditionally your maid (or matron if she is married) of honour would be your sister closest in age to you. If you don't have a sister or you aren't particularly close, it is perfectly alright to choose a friend instead. Likewise, if you are only having a couple of bridesmaids and don't feel comfortable choosing between them, why not get them to share the duties of maid of honour? The important thing is to choose people who will support you emotionally (I can't over-emphasise the importance of having a good listener on the phone when things get too much), be willing to help out with any tasks you ask of them, be honest with you and most of all, share your excitement about your big day.

Flower girls/Page boys

Flower girls and page boys are really just there to look cute. The flower girls normally carry a small posy or basket of flowers,

First things first!

or scatter petals in the bride's path as she walks down the aisle, and the page boy may carry the rings (otherwise this is the best man's responsibility). It is often a role assigned to a godchild, best friend's or relative's child, or more commonly these days, the bride and groom's own child.

Ushers

As with the bridesmaids, there is no rule as to how many ushers you should have and this is a useful role for placating any friends who may feel put out at not being chosen as best man. Again, consider what duties you will need your ushers to do and make sure that they are fully aware of these. They may just be required to hand out orders of service and see guests to their seats (if this is the case, and you are getting married in a very small chapel, any more than two will just get in each other's way), or you may need them to ensure that people are on the right coaches, get groups together for photographs, be in charge of music during the ceremony, etc. (if this is the case, relying on just two ushers would be unfair). Being an usher may seem like a small role, but in reality they can make the difference between a smooth-running event and a complete shambles – making sure everyone knows what is happening and are in the right place at the right time is an important task.

Father of the bride

The father of the bride has two traditional roles – to walk his daughter down the aisle to give her away, and to make a speech. If the father is not around, this role traditionally goes to the grandfather, older brother or other family member or close family friend. As with the best man, if you are to choose someone for the role, ensure it is someone who is comfortable giving a speech (although the pressure on the father of the bride to give a good speech is less than that of the best man) and someone who will keep you calm as you travel to the ceremony together. If you don't like the significance of your father 'giving' you to the groom, you may choose to walk down the aisle alone, or with both your parents, or even with the groom. It may be nice to include your father in the wedding preparations if you don't want him to feel left out, but generally fathers are happy to sit back and let you get on with it.

Mother of the bride

Traditionally the mother of the bride organised the entire wedding. Whilst this is no longer the case, many mothers will still want to be involved. Even if you have a mother who tries not to interfere (lucky you!) and leaves you to it, she will probably appreciate being asked to help and being included. If, on the other hand, you have a mother who wants to organise the whole thing, be sure to let your feelings and preferences be known from the outset – this is *your* wedding after all; don't get bullied into making decisions you don't want to. If your parents are paying for the whole wedding however, you will need to be diplomatic on this one and both parties will need to compromise.

The day itself will be a very emotional and proud day for your mother as well as for you and your fiancé – make sure she enjoys it and that she feels special too. Ensuring that one of the ushers makes it his duty to walk her to her seat and presenting her with a bouquet of flowers at the reception are just a couple of ways you can do this.

Other roles

If you want to include other special friends or family members outwith the wedding party, you could ask them to:

- act as a witness
- do a reading
- sing or play an instrument
- hand out favours
- say grace
- take photographs of the guests arriving, or during the evening
- help with any preparations – e.g. making invitations, favours, or the cake

First things first!

Who does what?

The following is a guideline of who normally does what, but feel free to reassign roles to the person or people that you think will do the better job.

Best Man
- Organises the stag night
- Collects clothing for the bridal party
- Collects and distributes boutonnières (buttonhole flowers) for the bridal party
- Ensures orders of service are taken to the ceremony
- Helps the groom to get ready on the morning of the wedding
- Looks after the rings
- Witnesses the signing of the register
- Gives speech and reads out messages
- Liaises with and pays minister/registrar/band/entertainers/DJ
- Ensures the return of any clothing, equipment, unopened drink
- Returns the marriage schedule to the Registration Office

Maid of Honour/Bridesmaids
- Organises the hen night
- Helps choose both the bride's and bridesmaids' dresses
- Helps choose shoes, accessories, flowers, and anything else
- Helps research bands, caterers, florists, and anything else
- Helps make favours, stationery, decorations, and anything else
- Acts as a shoulder to cry on and an emotional support to the bride
- Helps the bride to dress on the morning of the wedding
- Does a final check of the bride before she enters the ceremony
- Holds the bride's bouquet during the ceremony
- Witnesses the signing of the register
- Looks after any younger attendants
- Carries bride's emergency bag (see 'Showtime!' section)

Usher(s)

- See people to their seats for the ceremony
- Hand out Orders of Service
- Operate the CD system for ceremony/drinks reception
- Assist with guests' transport – to the ceremony, from the ceremony to the reception, and home at the end of the night
- Help the photographer round up groups for photographs
- Move flowers from ceremony to reception
- Light candles
- Put gifts in a safe place
- Ushers people from one part of the day to the next
- Collect up disposable cameras

How much?

Weddings are expensive, make no mistake about it. It doesn't help that whenever you mention the 'W' word, people seem to double the price of everything! It is essential, therefore, that you plan your budget carefully and try your best to stick to it. There is a table below to help you establish how much your overall budget will be, but work in a contingency amount as you will always overspend – it is difficult not to when you want the day to be absolutely perfect. The more particular you are and the more finishing touches you want, the more expensive your big day will be. However, the more organised you can be and the more research you are prepared to put in, the more savings you will be able to make. By getting three or four quotes for everything, searching on the web, shopping ahead in the sales, bartering, calling in favours, and even testing your creative skills by making some of the little extras by hand, you will be able to help keep those costs from spiralling out of control.

> ### Top Tip
> Get yourself a credit card that gives you air miles, and put everything you buy between now and your wedding on it. You may be able to cash in the air miles to help towards your honeymoon, or at least for a nice weekend break after you get back.

First things first!

Who pays for what?

Traditionally, the father of the bride paid for the entire reception, with the groom or father of the groom chipping in to help with things like transport and the rings. These days, with couples marrying later and earning more for themselves, it is becoming more customary for the happy couple to foot the bill themselves, albeit with a little help from their families. Only you will know what will work for you, whether either of your sets of parents are able, or willing, to help out or not. Make sure you discuss this early, though. You will need to know from the start how much money you have to play with – it will affect everything you organise, from the venue, to the catering, to the dress, and down to the favours.

Organising your finances

Before you can start looking at venues or trying on dresses, you will need to establish exactly how much money you have and how you are going to spend it – or alternatively how much money you need and where you're going to get it from! Every couple is different and the 'average' costs you will see in various bridal magazines should be taken with a pinch of salt. How can you give a bride an accurate 'guide cost' for a wedding dress? They can range from £200 to £10,000 or more! Do a bit of research based around the type of wedding you are thinking of – only you will know how extravagant your tastes are. Try to keep your feet on the ground though – yes, this is supposed to be the happiest day of your life, and yes, hopefully you will only do it once, but is it really worth being in debt for the next 10 years to fund it? Think about where you can compromise – is a fabulous dress the most important thing to you? Or would you rather thoroughly spoil all your friends with a magnificent meal at the reception that will have them talking for years? Do you really need that £500 chocolate fountain, or could you make do with a Marks and Spencer wedding cake? All brides have different priorities, and you will need to decide what yours are.

First things first!

Once you have done some research and worked out a ballpark budget, you can start to divide up your costs using the table below. Use the 'actual cost' column to keep track of your spending – if you overspend on your dress by £500 for example, you are going to have to try and save that back elsewhere. Another way of keeping tabs on your spending is to open a dedicated wedding account and/or credit card. Make sure you take out wedding insurance also; it doesn't cost very much but is well worth it for the additional peace of mind it provides you. There have been several stories in the press in recent years about venues burning down and dress or gift list companies going into liquidation, leaving many un-insured couples out of pocket.

Item	Estimated Cost	Actual Cost
Wedding rings	£	£
Minister/Registrar/Priest	£	£
Invitations/RSVP/Save the Date/Thank you cards	£	£
Orders of Service	£	£
Wedding dress	£	£
Accessories (veil, tiara, shoes, lingerie, jewellery)	£	£
Bridesmaids' dresses	£	£
Bridesmaids' accessories	£	£
Groom's outfit	£	£
Groomsmen's outfits	£	£
Flowers	£	£
Photographer	£	£
Videographer	£	£
Wedding cake	£	£
Wedding party transport	£	£
Guests' transport	£	£
Reception venue	£	£
Drinks reception	£	£

First things first!

Item	Estimated Cost	Actual Cost
Catering – including evening buffet	£	£
Drinks – champagne and wine	£	£
Bar tab	£	£
Table decorations – including menus and place cards	£	£
Favours	£	£
Room theming – including lighting/candles	£	£
First night accommodation	£	£
Band/DJ/entertainment	£	£
Fireworks	£	£
Wedding Insurance	£	£
	£	£
	£	£
10% contingency	£	£
TOTAL	£	£

Making it legal

Make sure you understand the legalities of getting married and are organised – the last thing you want is to have to postpone your wedding because your marriage notice form wasn't handed in on time or you didn't produce the correct documents.

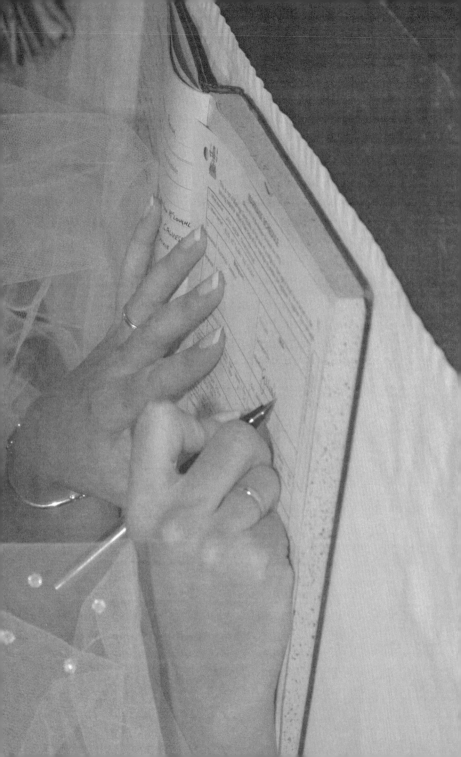

Making it legal

Who can be married in Scotland?

Any two persons, regardless of where they live, may marry in Scotland provided that:

- both persons are at least 16 years of age on the day of their marriage
- they are not related to one another in a way which would prevent their marrying
- they are unmarried (any person who has already been married must produce documentary evidence that the previous marriage has been ended by death, divorce or annulment)
- they are not of the same sex
- they are capable of understanding the nature of a marriage ceremony and of consenting to marrying
- the marriage would be regarded as valid in any foreign country to which either party belongs

Types of marriage

You can be married in either of two ways in Scotland – by a religious or by a civil ceremony:

- A religious marriage, which may take place anywhere, may be solemnised only by a minister, clergyman, priest or other person entitled to do so under the Marriage (Scotland) Act 1977
- A civil marriage, which may take place in a registration office or at an approved place, may be solemnised only by a registrar or an assistant registrar who has been authorised by the Registrar General for that purpose. You can obtain a list of approved places for the area in which you wish to be married from the registrar of births, deaths and marriages for that area. Alternatively, a list of approved places for Scotland can be obtained from the General Register Office for Scotland at the address at the end of the chapter.

Making it legal

Civil partnerships

As of 5 December 2005, The Civil Partnership Act 2004 came into force, allowing same sex couples to formally register their relationship. The registration of a civil partnership is secular in nature and therefore the legal formalities and any ceremony that the registrar agrees to perform must not contain any religious element. If you would like to have a religious ceremony or blessing, this can be arranged separately to the legal formalities of registering the civil partnership. A civil partnership may be registered only by a District Registrar or an Assistant Registrar who has been authorised by the Registrar General for this purpose. The registration of the civil partnership may take place in a registration office or in a place that the local authority agrees to. You should contact the local registrar for the district in which you wish to register the civil partnership for further details on available locations. Giving notice and the required documentation is similar to that for a marriage. You should refer to the information leaflet RCP1, which is available from the General Register Office for Scotland, for the full legal requirements for registering a civil partnership.

How and when to give notice

You can obtain a marriage notice form and information about fees from any registrar of births, deaths and marriages in Scotland.

- Each of you must complete and submit a marriage notice, along with the required documents (see below) and the appropriate fee, to the registrar for the district in which the marriage is to take place.

- Timing is important. The notices must be submitted early enough to enable the registrar to satisfy himself that you are free to marry one another. Normally notices should be in his hands about FOUR weeks before the marriage but if either or you have been married before, the notices should be with the registrar SIX WEEKS beforehand. The **minimum period is 15 days before the date of the proposed marriage**, but if you leave things as late as this you could be faced with the need to postpone your marriage.

- Only in exceptional circumstances will the Registrar General authorise a marriage to take place if 15 days' notice has not been given.

- Although you need not both attend personally at the registrar's office to hand in your marriage notice, at least one of you must attend there personally before the date of the marriage. This is necessary, in the case of a religious marriage, to collect the marriage schedule (see below) or, in the case of a civil marriage, to finalise arrangements with the registrar. Personal attendance is necessary at this stage because the registrar will need further information before the marriage can proceed.

- Every person giving notice is required to sign a declaration to the effect that the particulars and information given on the notice are correct. As a safeguard against bigamous marriages, a subsequent check of the information is made by the General Register Office for Scotland.

If you live in England or Wales

As an alternative to the normal procedure of giving notice to a registrar in Scotland, if you intend to marry

1. a person residing in Scotland, or
2. a person residing in England or Wales who has a parent residing in Scotland,

you may instead give notice of marriage to the superintendent registrar in the district of England or Wales in which you reside. The person you are marrying should, however, give notice in Scotland in the usual way.

- You should seek the advice of the superintendent registrar if you wish to proceed in this way. You should send the certificate for marriage obtained from him to the Scottish registrar as quickly as possible.

Documents to be produced

When giving or sending the marriage notice forms to the registrar each of you must supply the following:

Making it legal

- Your birth certificate
- If you have been married before and the marriage was dissolved, a certificate of divorce, or annulment or a certified copy decree. A decree of divorce granted outwith Scotland must be absolute or final – a decree nisi is not acceptable.
- If you are a widow or widower, the death certificate of your former spouse
- If you are domiciled in another country, outside the United Kingdom, a certificate of no impediment, issued by the competent authority, to the effect that you are free to marry (see below).
- If any of these documents is in a language other than English, a certified translation in English must also be produced.
- Do not delay giving notice simply because you are waiting for any of the documents mentioned above to come to hand. If time is getting short it is better to give notice first and then pass the documents to the registrar when they become available, but they must be made available to the registrar before the marriage. Provided the documents are in order the marriage can proceed as arranged.

If you are domiciled outside the United Kingdom

The normal procedure of giving notice to the registrar in Scotland must be followed but as previously mentioned an additional requirement is placed on you.

- If you are subject to the marriage laws of the country in which you live, you should obtain a certificate issued by the competent authority (usually the civil authority) to the effect that there is no impediment to your proposed marriage. If the certificate is in a language other than English, you should also produce a certified translation.
- In the absence of such a certificate without good reason being shown, it may not be possible for you to marry in Scotland.
- If you are now resident in the UK and have lived here for the last two years or more you need not submit such a certificate.

Making arrangements for the marriage ceremony

It is important to make early arrangements for the date and time of your marriage.

- If you are having a religious ceremony, contact the minister or clergyman who is to take the service before completing the notice of marriage.

- For a civil marriage, make advance arrangements with the registrar. This is particularly important if the ceremony is to be in a registration office or at an approved place in towns and cities, where large numbers of people want to be married at certain times of the year.

- Arrange for two persons, aged 16 years or over, to be present at your marriage to act as witnesses. They are required whether it is a religious or civil ceremony.

- Be sure to let the clergyman or the registrar know if you change your plans or decide to postpone your marriage.

The marriage schedule

When s/he is satisfied there is no legal impediment to the marriage, the registrar will prepare a marriage schedule from the information you have given him. The schedule is the most important document – **no marriage can proceed without it**.

- If you are having a religious marriage, the marriage schedule will be issued to you by the registrar. The schedule cannot be issued more than seven days before the marriage and the registrar will advise you when to call to collect it. The schedule cannot be collected on your behalf by a relative or friend – the registrar will issue it only to the prospective bride or bride-groom.

- The marriage schedule **must** be produced before a religious marriage ceremony to the person performing the marriage.

- Immediately after the ceremony, the schedule must be signed by both parties, by the person performing the marriage, and by the two witnesses. Thereafter it must be returned to the registrar so that he can register the marriage.

Making it legal

- If you are having a civil marriage, a marriage schedule will not be issued, but the registrar will have it available at the marriage ceremony. Subsequently s/he will register the marriage.
- A fee for the civil marriage and, if applicable, for the attendance of an authorised registrar at an approved place is payable to the registrar in advance.

Marriage certificate

After the marriage has been registered you can obtain copies of the marriage certificate from the registrar on payment of the appropriate fee.

The information provided here was taken from form RM1, available from the General Registrar Office for Scotland, and was correct at time of going to press.

For a more in depth guide, a directory of local registrars, a list of approved places for a civil marriage, or a guide to applicable fees, you can contact them at the address below, or see the government's website at www.gro-scotland.gov.uk

Marriage Section
General Register Office for Scotland
New Register House
3 West Register Street
Edinburgh
Scotland
EH1 3YT

Tel: 0131 314 4447
Fax: 0131 314 4532

E-mail: marriage@gro-scotland.gov.uk

Location! Location! Location!

Scotland offers a wealth of diverse venues from chic city hotels to romantic Highland castles. Whatever your vision for your wedding you are sure to find a venue to suit. And with Scotland's unique law on religious ceremonies and the recent law changes to civil ceremony licensing, the choice has never been better.

Location! Location! Location!

Even if you have your heart set on a particular venue, it is worth looking around a few others – even if it is only to confirm that you are making the right choice. You will glean ideas from other venues and their event co-ordinators, which you can use towards your wedding – even if you choose to go elsewhere.

Whether you are planning a church wedding followed by a knees-up in a barn, an outdoor civil ceremony followed by a garden party, or a religious ceremony followed by a formal banquet in a Highland castle, there are many points you will need to consider, before you draw up your shortlist of venues to visit:

Licence

As discussed in the 'Making it Legal' section, there are legal implications to be considered. If you want a civil ceremony, you will need to check that the venues you are considering have a licence for this.

Numbers

You will need to have an idea of your numbers before you start your search. It is no use setting your heart on an historic castle that can only seat 60 people for the ceremony if you are expecting 150 guests. Similarly, 20 guests will look lost in a banqueting hall designed to seat 250.

Location and accommodation

Will many of your guests be travelling from afar? If so, will it be easy for them to get to the venue from the airport or train station? If you are having different locations for the ceremony and reception, are they within a reasonable distance from each other? (I would recommend *never* more than an hour drive at most, and preferably no more than half an hour.) Can guests stay at the reception venue? Will it accommodate all your guests? Are there alternatives, possibly cheaper options nearby? Consider all these questions to ensure your guests feel as welcome and appreciated as possible.

Location! Location! Location!

Cost

If you are planning on taking exclusive hire of a castle for your big day, there will normally be a substantial hire fee for the privilege. Hotels, however, will often waive their function room fee if you can guarantee a minimum number of guests, as they make their money on the meal, bar takings and accommodation charges.

Many venues offer wedding packages and it is worth looking at them closely and carefully comparing them – no two are the same, which can make it difficult to establish which venue offers better value for money. One which looks outrageously expensive may, on closer inspection, offer you more for your money and ultimately work out cheaper than another which you originally thought to be less expensive. Whether the package includes the honeymoon suite, any decoration, a PA system or a Master of Ceremonies will make a large difference to your final bill. Other savings can be made with some venues. If the ceremony is to take place within the same venue as the reception, for example, you will not need to pay for transport between the two. Similarly if the venue you choose is in the city centre, you may not need to make arrangements for guests' transport, which will also help to keep your costs down. Use the guide below to help you to differentiate between the costs of different venues.

Calculating your venue cost

The following are worth considering when you are looking around your shortlisted venues. You may want to add other items depending on your requirements. Fill in the table for every venue you go to see and it will give you a more realistic comparison of costs:

Ceremonial room hire	£
Function suite hire	£
Wedding breakfast package	£
Drinks package	£

Location! Location! Location!

Welcome drink for evening guests	£
Evening buffet *	£
Table decorations	£
Additional room decoration/lighting	£
Honeymoon suite	£
Transport for bridal party	£
Coaches for guests	£
PA system – for background music/speeches	£
PA system/Organ for ceremony	£
TOTAL	£

* To calculate requirements for your evening buffet, divide the number of day guests by three and add this number to the number of evening guests.

Narrowing down your search

Once you have established your venue requirements, you will need to start looking around for any that suit your needs. One of the best one-stop sources of information for wedding venues in Scotland is the *Scottish Wedding Directory* – every issue comes with an updated venue guide, at the back of which is an easy to follow chart, dividing venues into areas of Scotland and with an at-a-glance guide to details such as maximum capacity, whether they have a marquee or a civil licence, number of bedrooms etc. This information can also be sourced on their website – www.scottishweddingdirectory.co.uk

Once you have narrowed down your search to five or six (or ten or twenty!) suitable venues, give them a call and request a brochure, have a look at their website and arrange to go and have a look around. This will enable you to get a feel for the place and its staff – ensure it has the right atmosphere to fit your vision and the staff to help you achieve this.

Location! Location! Location!

Don't underestimate the staff at a venue for their ability to help make your day run smoothly and make you feel special.
Many venues see weddings as one-in, one-out easy moneymaking:

A good venue events co-ordinator will listen to what you want, help make suggestions and be there on the day to ensure the smooth running of everything. They can be a great source of information for timings, the best locations for photographs, what decorations work best etc. If they can't understand that every little detail of the day is of vital importance to you, they're not doing their job properly and frankly, don't deserve your custom!

As you enter a venue, try to imagine the day as it unfolds, and walk around seeing it from your guests' point of view as well as your own. Where will people arrive? Where will the ceremony be? Where will you enter from? Where will the drinks reception be? Are there seats for any elderly people among your guests? Do you need to walk outside to get from one place to another? If so, does the venue provide umbrellas if it rains? Are there awkward steps to climb, which may affect elderly or disabled guests (or a bride in a long dress)? Where will the reception be held? Where will the band go? And the cake? Are the restrooms close to the function rooms and the bar?

'We arrived at one venue for a tour of the place. The events manager was seeing someone else when we arrived, even though we had made an appointment. When she finished with them and had seen them out the door, she turned to us and shouted 'Next!'. Even though it was done in a humorous manner, I knew that we wouldn't receive the personal attention we wanted to make our wedding day feel special. We didn't even bother to finish the tour.'

Kate

Look at colour schemes and see if they fit in with your vision of your big day. Hotel function suites invariably have big, swirly patterned carpets (they hide the dirt better!). However, don't be immediately put off – remember that there will be several tables with tablecloths and possibly a hundred chairs with people on covering that horrendous carpet so it will probably go unnoticed!

Top Tip

If possible, visit your venue at the same time of day and at the same time of year as your wedding day. This will give you an opportunity to check things such as room temperature and light, and may make apparent any problems, such as an icy path leading to the church, parking problems etc. It's all very well envisaging a candlelit ceremony when you visit the venue in the dead of winter, but not so good when you turn up for your summer wedding and there is sun streaming through the window, ruining that romantic ambience!

Have an idea of the type of wedding you want before you go so that you can imagine if it will fit in with the venue. It will also affect the type of questions you will need to ask. For example, if you envisage a candlelit meal for your wedding breakfast, you will need to check that the venue allows candles. Don't feel awkward about asking as many questions as you want and writing down the answers – it will help you to go over the pros and cons of each venue once you have seen them all if you have something to refer to when you get home. Below are some sample questions to ask each venue you visit. Type them up on a piece of paper per venue with gaps for your answers and keep them all together to refer to once you have visited them all. This list is just to get you started. Think about your wedding individually and what is important to you and add your own questions to this list.

Questions to ask... the venue

- What is included in the wedding package?
- Does it include hire of all tables, chairs, linen, crockery, glassware etc? What colour are they?
- Is it possible to request different colours/styles and what will the charge be for this?

Location! Location! Location!

- Do you have high chairs?
- Are you flexible with menu choices? Can we make suggestions?
- Can we sample the menus/wines? Is there a charge for this?
- Do you provide an evening buffet? Are you flexible with choice? What is the cost per person?
- Can we bring our own wine/champagne? What is the corkage charge?
- Can we have a copy of the bar tariff?
- What is the location of the ceremony/drinks reception/wedding breakfast?
- Can we have the ceremony/drinks outside? What is the alternative if it rains?
- What is the maximum capacity for the ceremony?
- What is the maximum capacity for a dinner dance?
- What is the maximum capacity for the evening reception?
- Can we decorate the room ourselves? Are there any restrictions?
- What access times are we (and suppliers) allowed for set-up/breakdown?
- What is the usual table layout? Where does the top table go?
- What is the usual position of the cake table? Do you supply cake stand and knife?
- Do the guests need to leave the room in order to turn it around for the evening dance?
- Where would they go while this is happening?
- How big is the dance floor? Is there adequate staging for a band?
- What facility do you have for music playback or speeches? (eg. PA system, organ for ceremony)
- What capacity of power do you have? (This will be important for lighting, band etc.)
- Does the room/marquee have heating/air conditioning?

- What time is the bar licensed until? Is it possible to extend this?
- Is there a cloakroom? Is it attended? Is there a safe place for gifts?
- Is there disabled access?
- Is there ample parking?
- Are there adequate toilet facilities?
- Is there a private room for changing?
- Do you have on-site accommodation? Do you have special rates for wedding guests?
- What is your booking and payment policy?

What's your style?

Castle

What could be more fairytale romantic than getting married in a Scottish castle? It is the idea of a castle wedding with all the associated history and tradition that attracts thousands of happy couples to Scotland every year.

Location! Location! Location!

There are many different types of castle in Scotland, from derelict monuments to grand hotels. They needn't be ridiculously expensive either, although you will generally need to pay a hire fee on top of all your catering costs as you will probably take exclusive use of the castle. The one set back of castle weddings is that castles tend to be smaller than you would imagine – this means that for a larger wedding, the reception generally takes place in a marquee in the grounds, although you can still make the most of the castle atmosphere for your ceremony and drinks reception, and it will undoubtedly provide an amazing backdrop for photos. Unless the castle is functioning as a hotel, it is unlikely that there will be enough bedrooms to accommodate all your guests so alternative accommodation will need to be sourced. Bear in mind also that if the castle you choose is run by either Historic Scotland or the National Trust for Scotland, it is likely to be open to the public during the day so you will need to organise your timings around this.

Church

Although less common than it once was, a church wedding is still a popular choice, especially with the more traditional brides. It is obviously a more cost effective option too, as you don't need to pay a venue hire fee (although you will still need to pay a contribution, especially if you are not a regular member of the parish). Churches tend to be large enough to seat all your wedding guests, and all the seating, organ and PA system will already be in place. You will need to contact the local parish minister directly to arrange your wedding, and contact details for the different denominations can be found in the directory at the back of this book.

Hotel

There are hundreds of hotels all over Scotland that can cater for your wedding. For the ultra-stylish and hip amongst you, new boutique hotels are popping up all over our cities, or for the more traditional bride, there is an abundance of elegant country estate hotels to choose from. For a hotel wedding, there is the obvious advantage that your guests can stay overnight at the venue (which

Location! Location! Location!

has the added bonus that they can stay and party until the wee hours in the residents' bar if they wish!), there will be a room for you to change in, and you won't need to worry about transporting everyone home at the end of the night.

Restaurant/Pub

If you have a favourite restaurant or pub, why not hire it out for your big day? You will be guaranteed good food and will already have an idea of the ambience of your venue, in addition to the level of service provided. Scotland has a wealth of good restaurants and bars, from the cheap and cheerful, to the very traditional, to the chic and not-so-cheap, so you will definitely not be stuck for choice.

Regal Grandeur

How about a stately home? Think ballrooms with magnificent chandeliers, ornate pillars, oak panelled dining rooms, the bride drawing up in a horse and carriage… weddings don't get much more grand than this and there are plenty of elegant venues in Scotland, which can help this dream become reality.

Marquee

A marquee offers the ultimate in choice and flexibility. You could pitch one in your back garden, or a friendly farmer's field, or in the grounds of a fabulous castle that can't quite accommodate your numbers. Many castles and hotels will be able to organise a marquee for you, or put you in touch with a reliable supplier. If you are going it alone, and are erecting a marquee on private ground, you will have your work cut out... there is a lot to organise, which you would normally take for granted at any other venue. You will need to find your own caterer, hire furniture, kitchen equipment, arrange a water supply, organise drink, obtain a bar licence, ensure you have adequate staging for entertainment, a PA system, a generator – and that's all before you think about theming and decorating the marquee! You will also need to take advice from the marquee company that the location is suitable – and not somewhere that is prone to flooding, or severe gale force winds! If you do have the time and energy to organise all this, then it really is the ultimate way to have complete control over every aspect of your day (except, that is, the weather!).

Registration Office

Until April 2002, all civil ceremonies had to take place in a registration office. As this is no longer the case, registration office weddings are on the decline. They still offer a low-key, informal setting for a wedding however and require very little preparation (although on the reverse side of this coin, you can do very little to personalise the venue).

More unusual venues

For the less traditional amongst you, how about a stationary carriage at the Funicular Railway on CairnGorm Mountain, followed by a reception at the Base Station? Or what about tying the knot underwater with the sharks at Deep Sea World in North Queensferry? A bit too radical? Perhaps the Royal Botanic Garden, Edinburgh will be more to your taste, where you can have your ceremony outside amongst the trees, followed by drinks in the tropical hothouse or on the lawns and the reception in Caledonian Hall. For a more intimate affair, the vaulted cellars of Marlin's Wynd in the centre of Edinburgh's Old Town offers an atmosphere that's hard to beat. Perhaps a wedding aboard a paddle steamer on Loch Katrine is more your thing, or, for the ultimate in romance, take a look at Corsewall Lighthouse Hotel, on Scotland's West Coast, near Stranraer. With views across the Irish Sea, this offers a unique wedding venue that is sure to have people reminiscing for years to come! The world (or rather Scotland) is your oyster – dare to be different, go forth, explore!

I do!

*Take time in the planning of your ceremony.
Most people look forward to the party and celebrations,
but remember that it is during the ceremony that the
actual marriage takes place. You will want it to be
memorable, and personal to you as a couple.*

I do!

Civil or Religious?

This is the first decision you will need to make about your ceremony. Remember that in Scotland you can have a religious ceremony anywhere, provided you can find a minister who is willing to marry you. For a civil ceremony, you must get married in a registry office or a venue that has been granted a civil licence. If you have already chosen your venue, you may not have a choice as to what type of ceremony you can have. For more about this, see the 'Making it Legal' chapter.

Finding a Minister/Priest/Registrar

Once you have chosen your venue you will need to find a minister or registrar who will perform the marriage ceremony – unless you decide to marry in a church or registry office where this shouldn't be necessary.

If you decide on a religious ceremony outwith a church you will need to arrange for a minister or clergyman to perform the ceremony. If you are a member of a parish, you could ask your local minister if he would be willing to perform the ceremony – it may be nice to have somebody who knows you personally. It will depend on the minister however as some do not like to perform marriage ceremonies outwith the church. If you are marrying at a venue away from where you live, ask the venue to suggest a minister as they often have a list of suitable ministers on their books. Alternatively you can contact the religious body directly. Useful addresses can be found in the Directory section.

If you opt for a civil ceremony you will need to contact the local Registrar Office in the district in which you plan to marry. A directory of registrars in Scotland can be found on the General Registrar Office for Scotland website.

I do!

Music

The music you choose will depend on the style of your wedding –
traditional or modern, religious or civil, and whether you have any
themes into which you can incorporate your music. There are
obviously practical implications to consider such as whether there
is room for a choir or musicians and, of course, your budget. If you
are having a civil ceremony, you cannot have any music that has
any religious connotations, and if you are having a religious
ceremony, you will need to get approval from the minister for
your music choices.

Prelude

It is a good idea to have some music playing for when your guests
are waiting for you to arrive. Think of your groom – he will be very
nervous standing at the front of the room and a silent room with
everybody whispering will only add to his nerves! You can decide
whether you would prefer to have an organist, live musicians, or
recorded music.

Entrance

This is your big day and here is your chance to make your entrance!
Something rousing and dramatic is normally appropriate and
guaranteed to get the ladies' tears flowing as you sweep through the
doorway! If you are having a piper at your wedding, traditionally
he should pipe you in and as you walk down the aisle.

Some of the more popular entrance tunes:

Arrival of the Queen of Sheba	(Handel)
Ave Maria	(Schubert)
Bridal March	(Wagner)
Crown Imperial	(Walton)
Music for a Royal Fireworks	(Handel)
Hallelujah Chorus	(Handel)
Jesu, Joy of Man's Desiring	(JS Bach)
New World Symphony	(Dvořák)

Ode to Joy	(Beethoven)
Water Music	(Handel)
Wedding Cantata No 22	(JS Bach)
Wedding March	(Mendelssohn)
Canon in D	(Pachelbel)

Hymns

If you are having a religious ceremony, you can decide whether to have hymns or not. It is up to you to choose hymns which you particularly like but try to choose hymns that people will know – especially these days when fewer people go to church regularly – there is nothing more awkward than the minister and your mother being the only singers in the congregation! If you are marrying in a very large church with only a few guests, it may also be worth hiring the church choir to help out with the singing, rather than have a few embarrassed voices desperately trying to fill the room. Check the words carefully and make sure that there is nothing in them that is inappropriate for a wedding. You can usually cut verses out of a hymn too if there are several – check with the minister. It is usual to have two to three hymns. The first is sung at the beginning of the ceremony, after the minister has welcomed everybody. The final hymn is often more celebratory and lively and is sung after the official marriage has taken place, and before the wedding schedule is signed.

Some of the more popular wedding hymns:

All Things Bright and Beautiful
Amazing Grace
Bind Us Together
Dear Lord and Father of Mankind
Give Me Joy in My Heart
I Danced in the Morning (also known as *Lord Of The Dance*)
I Vow to Thee My Country
Immortal Invisible God Only Wise
Love Divine All Loves Excelling

I do!

Make Me a Channel of Your Peace
Morning Has Broken
O Jesus I Have Promised
One More Step Along the World I Go
Praise My Soul the King of Heaven
The Lord's My Shepherd I'll Not Want

Signing the marriage schedule

Whilst you disappear to sign the marriage schedule (or even if this is done in view of your guests), there are a few minutes where your guests will be sitting waiting. It is a good idea to have some form of music so that they are either entertained, or don't feel awkward about talking amongst themselves. Again you have a number of choices – the organist could play an additional music piece, or perhaps you know someone with a talent for Spanish guitar or the violin who could entertain the congregation? Or someone who can sing a solo? Or maybe you could have another hymn.
Or alternatively, this is a nice time to play a song that is personal to the bride and groom, as the formal part of the ceremony is over and everyone can begin to relax.

The processional/retiral music

This is played after the bride and groom have signed the marriage schedule and as everyone leaves the room and should be a joyous piece of music appropriate to the occasion. There are several classical pieces that are commonly used, (see entrance tunes above) but again you can be creative and choose something more contemporary to get everyone in the mood for the celebrations ahead.

As with everything – there is no hard and fast rule when it comes to your music. Music is very subjective and can be used to create the atmosphere you want and really personalise your wedding.

Readings

Readings can personalise your ceremony as much as the music, so look through books and magazines, search the web and choose them with care. Remember that the more popular readings, although beautiful and rousing, can become overused and if yours is the fifth wedding that your guests are attending that year, the reading may begin to lose its poignancy.

If you are having a civil ceremony you will not be able to have any readings with religious content and if you are having a religious ceremony you will need to get approval from your minister before you finalise your choices. There are so many readings to choose from, from the very traditional to the very modern, and you can choose them from the Bible, a favourite poem, lyrics to a favourite song, an extract from a novel or, of course you can write your own. The internet is a very useful source of material. Below is a selection of different styles of readings, to give you some inspiration.

Lucky horseshoe

A silver horseshoe is traditionally presented to the bride by a pageboy or other child, as she leaves the church on the arm of her new husband. This is to hang outside their marital home to bring them luck. The story behind this is as follows: In the tenth century St Dunstan, who was also a blacksmith, was one day approached by a man who asked that horseshoes be attached to his cloven feet. St Dunstan immediately recognised the man as the Devil and told him that in order to carry out his task he would need to shackle the Devil to the wall. He then carried out the task making it as painful as possible so that the Devil begged for mercy. St Dunstan refused to release him until the Devil promised that he would never enter the house of a Christian. He would be able to tell if the household were of Christian beliefs by the horseshoe hanging above the door to the house.

I do!

Biblical readings

There are many passages in the bible suitable for weddings. Below are some popular choices.

Corinthians 13:1-13: 'If I speak in the tongues of men and of angels, but have not love... And now these three remain: faith, hope and love. But the greatest of these is love.'

Ephesians 4: 25-32: 'Therefore, having laid aside falsehood... just as God in Christ also forgave you.'

1 John 4:7-21: 'Dear Friends, let us love one another... Whoever loves God must also love his brother.'

Ecclesiastes 4:9-12: 'Two are better than one... two will withstand him.'

Song of Solomon 2:8-16: 'Listen! My Lover! Look!... My lover is mine and I am his; he browses among the lilies.'

Genesis 2:15-25: 'The Lord God took the man and put him in the Garden of Eden... The man and his wife were both naked, and they felt no shame.'

Poetry recommendations

Shakespeare is a popular choice for wedding readings, but bear in mind that not everybody feels comfortable reading Shakespeare or can do it justice, so choose your readers carefully! Sonnet 116, *Let me not to the marriage of true minds* is a popular choice. Other popular poems include the following:

How Do I Love Thee? by Elizabeth Barrett Browning

The Good-Morrow by John Donne

Because She Would Ask Me Why I Loved Her by Christopher Brennan

First Love by John Clare

A Birthday by Christina Rosetti

He Wishes For the Cloths of Heaven by W B Yeats

The Promise by Eileen Rafter

Or for a more Scottish feel to the ceremony, how about some Robert Burns? However Burns, like Shakespeare requires a certain skill to recite it properly. *My Love is like a Red, Red Rose* is a popular choice. Other popular Scottish readings include *Fond Lovers in July* by Alf T Matthews and *O'er the Muir Amang the Heather* by Jean Glover.

Modern readings

Many modern brides are choosing to avoid the traditional readings in favour of more contemporary readings with practical advice for your lives together: *Art of Marriage* (Anon), *Keys of Love* by Robert M Millay, *A Marriage Prayer* by Bud Henry Bowen and *Blessing For a Marriage* by James Dillet Freeman are all favourites.

Or perhaps you have a favourite book in which you have found a suitable reading (see Shakespeare's *Romeo and Juliet*, Diane Ackerman's *A Natural History of Love*, and Louis de Berniere's *Captain Corelli's Mandolin*).

Readings for children

There are lots of readings suitable for children with Edward Lear's *The Owl and the Pussycat*, extracts from *The Velveteen Rabbit* by Margery Williams, and A A Milne's *Winnie the Pooh* being particularly popular. For a younger child, something shorter like *Hug of War* by Shel Silverstein might be more appropriate.

It's your ceremony and you should personalise it as much as you like so that it really means something to you as a couple.

Who wears what and how

Obviously you will be a vision of beauty in your fantastic wedding dress... but what about the rest of the wedding party? Trying to co-ordinate three bridesmaids of different shapes and sizes with a groom, a best man and three ushers can be a challenge for anyone... and just how do you wear those Ghillie Brogues?!

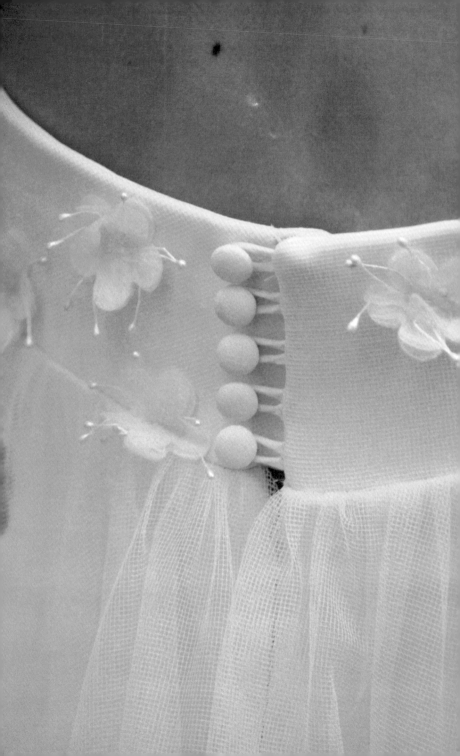

Who wears what and how

The Bride

The dress

So, we come to the dress… the one you have been dreaming about since you were a little girl! No matter what your style is, everyone wants to look like a million dollars on their wedding day and these days the pressure really is on. Nobody wants a 'meringue', but with all the designs now going for 'understated elegance', how do you find something really unique that will make you dazzle on your big day? One of the biggest challenges facing brides these days is that, unless we belong to a society that regularly attends charity balls and black-tie affairs, we rarely wear dresses, especially of the long and flowing type, so how do we know what style will really suit us and make people stop and stare?

There are several books and endless magazine articles which will advise you on what dress style will suit your shape – but honestly? The only way to really know is to try – try, try, try. You may have an idea in your head of how you imagine your dress to be, but still – try different designs, you may be surprised. Chances are you will never have worn a full-skirted gown with underskirts and the whole shebang. Of course, there may be a very good reason for this but until you try it on, you don't know how it will look! Wedding magazines are full of pages and pages of dresses – by all means purchase all the magazines and pore over the pages to get an idea of which designers you like, but until you try the dresses on yourself, you won't know.

The shopping trip

You will often read advice telling brides that the way to shop for a dress is to go on your own, try on all the different styles, and then take someone along with you to see your shortlisted choices. I disagree… your wedding dress is likely to be one of the singularly most expensive items of clothing you will ever buy – and probably the most exciting too. Surely it deserves a bit more pomp and ceremony than wandering around the shops on your own as if you were looking for another business suit!

Who wears what and how

So go on, make a day of it! Take your bridesmaids, a trusty friend, or even your mother and use this as an excuse to live out your *Sex and the City* fantasies – make time for lunch, have your nails done and then end the day with cocktails – you'll feel well and truly pampered and fussed over and it's a great form of female bonding! Many bridal boutiques also stock bridesmaids' dresses – it'll be more of a giggle if they try on things too, and will make them feel more included. Just be careful who you choose to take along, as you don't want anyone who will be too overpowering and bully you into trying on dresses you don't want to.

How it works

When you try on dresses in bridal salons, you are actually trying on samples of each design. Once you have chosen 'the one', your measurements will be taken and the dress ordered in your size. You will be required to make a deposit of around 50% and it will then take approximately 12 to 14 weeks (allow 16 to be safe) for your dress to be delivered, at which time you will need to make another appointment for a fitting. Remember to check with the salon when you order your dress whether additional fittings will incur further costs. One thing to note: ridiculously, many bridal salons only stock dresses up to a size 14. If you are a size 16 or larger, it is advisable to enquire beforehand and unfortunately you may have to try on dresses with them open at the back… not very accommodating, I know!

'I found myself in a bridal boutique, on my own, trying on dresses… The shop assistant stuck a veil on my head, and there I was in the mirror – a BRIDE! I looked fantastic and I had no-one to share the moment with except a shop assistant I had met a few minutes ago! After that I refused to go into any other shops until I had organised for my bridesmaids to be there with me.'

Natalie

Hiring

If you're not the kind of person who wants to keep your dress in the wardrobe to pass down the generations, perhaps you will consider hiring? Hiring can give you the opportunity to wear a much more expensive dress than you could usually afford, although obviously your choice will be more limited.

Having it designed

So you've looked around all the salons and have a pretty good idea of what you want, but can't quite find 'the one'? Then it's time to find a designer. Many people consider this to be a luxury they just can't afford, but when the majority of shops make each dress to measure anyway, you'll often find that the difference in price is less than you would imagine. A lesser-known local designer will often be able to design you something to your specification for less than buying a well-known designer dress off the peg. The process can be fun and you will end up with a one-of-a-kind dress, exactly as you dreamt.

However, be warned – if you are not used to having clothes made, it can be stressful! When you buy a dress from a shop, you have the opportunity to 'try before you buy', a luxury you are obviously not granted when having something designed as a one-off. Check the process with your designer – many will make the dress up in a cheap fabric first to allow you to see the dress shape and make any changes. They then use this mocked-up dress (called a toile) to make the pattern for the actual dress.

For your first consultation, go armed with ideas of what you want, pictures from magazines of dresses which have caught your eye, and take samples of fabrics which you particularly like. Make sure the designer spends time listening to you and work with him or her to come up with a design that you are really happy with.

Be prepared to be flexible and take advice from the designer, after all they spend their time keeping an eye on fashion and will be able to make good suggestions:

Who wears what and how

They may also be able to make good suggestions for ways of adapting the dress for use after the wedding. However, if you really do know what you want, don't let a designer talk you out of it. If they don't share your vision, go elsewhere, and find someone who does.

> *I spent hours looking for a dress to jump out at me. When I couldn't find it I went to a designer with a pretty fixed idea of what I wanted the dress to look like, but somehow it didn't match the image I was trying to portray. After an hour of talking round in circles and several sketches later, he came up with exactly what I was looking for – nothing like what I had originally tried to describe, but incorporating all my ideas to achieve something far sexier and completely unique!*
>
> Michelle

Something more traditional?

Perhaps you're looking for something more traditionally 'Scottish'? This doesn't have to mean a full-on tartan dress (though of course it can be, if that's what you want). There are designers who specialise in Celtic and medieval designs, or you could go for a more subtle approach and have a bodice with Celtic embroidered designs (which you will find on many dresses these days), a tartan ribbon, or a tartan trim to the bodice. You can then mirror the detail on the rest of your bridal party outfits.

Surprise!

However much you love your dress, try to resist the temptation to tell everyone about it! (Although nearly everyone will ask!) Your dress is the main thing that you should keep as a surprise from everybody.

Don't ruin the surprise – it will make people all the more appreciative of you on the day!

Who wears what and how

> *'Whenever I go to a friend's wedding, one of my favourite parts is seeing the bride for the first time as she walks through the church doors – and seeing how beautiful she looks and what her dress is like.'*

Lynne

Top Tips

- Make appointments before you go shopping – it will allow the assistants to dedicate their time to you

- Don't feel pressured to find 'the one' on the first day shopping – use this as a chance to find out what styles suit you, and to narrow down your search

- Try on as many styles as you can, even those that you don't think will suit you

- Listen to advice from the shop assistants – after all they have the experience to be able to help

- At the same time, don't let them pressure you into making a decision you don't want to – if you are at all unsure, go away and think about it – you can always go back

- Think practically – try sitting, walking and dancing in the dress. If you choose a dress with a train, see if it can be detachable or ask about having a button and loop fitted so that you can hook it up for the evening's festivities

- Ask if the salon has any shoes you can try on with the dress; heels alter your posture, and therefore the way the dress looks

- Be organised – remember dresses can take up to 16 weeks to arrive and then will need to be fitted – the last thing you want is to be panicking that it won't be ready on time and there may be additional costs involved in rush-jobs

- Make sure you have your shoes and wedding lingerie with you for your final fitting – they will alter your shape and posture

Who wears what and how

Top Tips

- Ask for swatches of the material from your dress – they will help when choosing your shoes, accessories, flowers etc.

- Watch that diet! If you are planning to lose weight before your wedding, be sure to let the shop assistant or designer know. But never, ever order a dress in a smaller size with the hope that you will fit into it by the big day!

- Have someone with you for the final fitting who will be there with you as you get ready on the wedding day. I know one bride who was twenty minutes late because nobody knew how to lace her into her dress properly!

- Ensure whoever buttons you into your dress is not wearing coloured nail polish – it will come off on the dress, no matter how dry it is.

Money wise!

- Be realistic and don't get too carried away – at the end of the day it is just a dress and you will only wear it once!

- Know your budget before you go and don't try on anything too far outwith it... what if you fall in love with a dress that's £3,000 above your budget and then you don't find anything that compares?

- Don't go way over your budget with the idea that you will be able to sell the dress and make half the money back again – it may not sell or may get damaged – if you can sell it later, fine – but see this as a bonus, not part of your budget!

- If you are considering selling your dress after the big day – enquire into doing this either before, or as soon as possible after your wedding as fashion trends move quickly and it may soon become dated

- Check with your salon whether they charge for additional fittings once the dress arrives

Who wears what and how

- If you really can't (or won't) justify spending the expected price for a wedding dress – have a look on the high street – shops such as Monsoon and Debenhams stock beautiful gowns at a fraction of the price. As long as you stick to white/ivory you shouldn't be in danger of dressing the same as one of your guests!

- Another option is to look at bridesmaid dresses – these often come in white too and are also a fraction of the price of a wedding dress

- Customise... if you are at all creative (or know someone who is), how about buying a dress from the high street and customising it with beads, sequins, feathers, flowers etc. to achieve your dream?

- Consider hiring a dress or a buying a second-hand dress – it may mean that you can afford to wear an otherwise unattainable dress

- Sales shopping – end of season sales are a good time to buy ex-samples from bridal shops – these tend to be in January and July.

Looking after your dress

- Hang it up on a padded hanger as soon as you get it home

- Get advice on pressing your dress if you think it will need it on the morning of the wedding, it will save any burning accidents!

- Brush any confetti off your dress as soon as possible – it may stain if it gets wet

- Deal with any spills immediately to minimise the chances of permanent staining

- Have your dress professionally cleaned as soon after the wedding as possible – it is expensive but don't be tempted to skip this, thinking you will never wear it again – moths love dirty clothes!

- Check it once a year to ensure there is no damage (what the hell, why not try it on once a year just for the fun of it and relive your wedding day memories!)

Who wears what and how

Accessories

Veil

To wear a veil or not to wear a veil? That is the question! A lot of modern brides feel a veil is too traditional, and decide against wearing one. However, with the style of wedding dresses becoming more sleek and elegant and less 'meringue-like', a veil can really set you apart as the bride. Once you have chosen your dress – try one. They come in all different lengths from shoulder-length to cathedral length, which drags along the ground behind you. And they can be finished with beads, pearls or embroidery to complement your dress. Every person and every dress suits something different – so have fun trying on a few. If you decide it is not for you, not to worry – there are lots of other options.

Traditionally the veil was worn to protect the bride from evil spirits and as a symbol of chastity and modesty, with the top layer over the bride's face as she walked up the aisle. Her father would then lift it up, in order to present her to her new husband – or it was even left in place until after they had been announced husband and wife. As the modern bride tends to wear her veil as an accessory to her dress, rather than as a means to protect her innocence, this is rarely done these days. However, if you are a hopeless romantic you may like the idea of your new husband being the first to see your face, rather than the last (as everyone else has seen you walk down the aisle) and you could have him lift your veil as you arrive at the altar. If you do decide on this approach, make sure your bridesmaid is on hand and well briefed to make sure it lies flat after he has done this, rather than have it sticking out throughout the entire ceremony.

> *I wanted a really modern look for my wedding day and thought a veil would be too traditional. However, when I tried one on with my dress, I was blown away – it looked amazing, it really finished the look – all my bridesmaids and my mum started to cry and I knew I had to wear it!*
>
> Sarah

Who wears what and how

Top Tip

Hang your veil in a steamy bathroom to get rid of any creases, as it will easily burn with an iron.

Tiara

The ultimate bridal accessory – you can't get more girly than a sparkly tiara! There are some really beautiful tiaras out there and they come in all shapes and colours... gold, silver, with pearls, Swarovski crystals, feathers – you name it, you can find it. Many bridal salons sell these so you can try them on when trying dresses and many designers make them to match their dresses. Look for one that will complement the detail of your dress if possible – for example if you have Swarovski crystals on your bodice, reflect this in your tiara. Try on different sizes and shapes to see which suits you best and try it further forward or further back on your head until it looks right. Remember to take it along with you for your hair trial also to see how it will look. Alternatively you could go for a crown, à la Victoria Beckham – but it takes a certain type of dress (and a certain type of bride) to carry off this look.

Other options

Not a veil and tiara kind of gal? Don't despair – it's the 21st century and anything goes! Look at the fashion pages in bridal magazines for some inspiration. Talk to your florist about flowers for your hair – this doesn't have to be a full crown of flowers, a single striking flower pinned into your hair or tiny little rose buds placed amongst a messy up-do is a more subtle and contemporary look. Or check out Cherry Chau's range of feather hair accessories and sparkly clips, available at Harvey Nichols and Selfridges, for the ultimate in funky modern style. For cheaper high street options, try Accessorise, Claire's Accessories and clothes shops such as Oasis and Topshop.

Who wears what and how

Jewellery

At the beginning of your wedding day, you will be wearing your engagement ring on your right hand (to leave your second finger on your left hand free for the wedding ring – the engagement ring then goes on top of this). It is nice to leave the rest of your fingers free of rings as everyone (well, all the girls!) will want to admire your new ring and you don't want to detract from it. It is often said of wedding day jewellery that less is more – however a current trend is for a simple dress that is accessorised with more elaborate jewellery. Necklaces that cover the entire neck and then drape down onto the breastbone, worn with a strapless dress is a very contemporary look. Again, look for inspiration in bridal magazines and see what works best with your dress.

Many brides feel that their overall look will be better without a watch. However, if you are used to wearing a watch, wear one. It will drive you mad if you are continually wondering what time it is, or if the day suddenly comes to an end when you weren't expecting it to. If your current watch doesn't go with your wedding look, high street fashion stores such as Oasis and Next do very reasonably priced fashion watches.

Lingerie

Your wedding is an ideal excuse to buy yourself some sassy sexy underwear. Before you make a beeline for Agent Provocateur however, you will need to ensure that what you buy will complement your dress, in shape and colour… there is no point spending all that money on a stunning dress to ruin the line of it with the wrong size bra and a VPL! The first thing you should do is get yourself professionally measured – the majority of women wear the wrong size bra and most of the time it shows too. Most shops specialising in lingerie will offer a fitting service and you would be well advised to use it. Even if you have been measured before, you may have changed size, especially if you have lost any weight in the lead-up to your wedding day. A professional will also be able to advise on the best type of underwear for the style of your dress and the look you are trying to achieve – bigger cleavage, smaller cleavage, flatter tummy, shapelier bum etc. Lingerie can be very clever these days! Choose the colour and detail carefully too – if it is too white, it may show under an ivory dress and even if it is the right colour, the pretty lace decoration on it may show through a sheer dress.

Just remember – if you end up having to buy flesh coloured seamless underwear with a tummy panel that doesn't exactly scream 'sexy bride alert' then you can always slip into something more alluring later!

Shoes

You will pretty much be on your feet all day, whether you are dancing or circulating to ensure you talk to everyone. So number one priority for your shoes is comfort. If you are a real shoe fiend (and most girls are!) this could be your chance to really splash out à la Carrie Bradshaw and buy those Manolo Blahnik's – after all when else will you justify spending that kind of money on a pair of shoes? However, back down to earth – remember that they will likely be hidden underneath your dress for most of the day and really, think back to the weddings you have been to... can you really remember the shoes the bride was wearing?

There are several shops that specialise in bridal shoes, or check out high street shoe shops around the Christmas party season for funky, sparkly shoes perfect for complementing a wedding dress. If you can't find any quite the right colour, there are several shops offering a shoe-dying service – take along a swatch of material from your dress and they will match it. Rainbow Club offer a bespoke shoe service, where they will make shoes

Who wears what and how

to match your dress – especially useful if you are going for an unusual fabric. Try to be organised and get your shoes as early as possible – you will need them for your final dress fitting and it is a good idea to wear them around the house a few times before the big day to wear them in a bit (slip a sock over them if you are worried about getting them dirty). Remember too that feet swell when they get hot and sweaty, so it may be an idea to buy shoes that are slightly too big. You can wear an insole during the day and then take it out once you hit the dancefloor!

Something old, something new, something borrowed, something blue

This is one tradition that the modern bride still likes to follow when dressing for her wedding day, even if just out of irrational superstition!

Something old: represents a link between the bride and her old life – perhaps a piece of her mother's or grandmother's jewellery

Something new: represents good fortune and success in her new life – usually her wedding dress, or any other item of her attire

Something borrowed: this should be borrowed from a happily married woman to bring good luck to her own marriage – it could be an item of clothing, jewellery or even a handkerchief

Something blue: blue traditionally represented purity and fidelity – this is often worn in the form of a blue-trimmed garter, or a blue ribbon sewn on the inside of the dress hem

Bridesmaids

There are lots of grey areas when it comes to bridesmaids. Who pays for the dresses? Who pays for the accessories? Who decides what they wear? Do they all have to wear the same thing?

I think it is only polite that if you are dictating what they should wear (and even if you don't *dictate* as such, you will probably be choosing something that will tie in with the whole look of your wedding rather than just telling them to wear what they like) then you should pay for it. It is up to you who pays for the accessories, and it will depend on how much control you want over the whole look. Perhaps you could just buy the shoes and let them decide how much more they want to dress it up. Generally speaking – the more of a say you have, the more you pay.

So who does decide what they wear? Assuming that you have chosen your bridesmaids because they are your friends, you should treat them as such. Listen to whether they have any preferences or hang-ups – perhaps one of them is particularly paranoid about the tops of her arms or has eczema on her back? Look at them as a group – are they all a similar size, shape and colour? Will the same style suit them all? If they are very different, perhaps you could choose a colour and let each of them choose their own style... they can have a uniform 'look' without being identical. Imagine the *Sex and the City* girls as bridesmaids – four bridesmaids, four bridesmaid dresses – all the same colour, but with each girl's personality clearly depicted. This can be a particularly helpful approach if you have different age groups and you don't really want your 12 year old niece in the same sexy shift dress your 26 year old best friend is wearing! Or for a different approach – why not have the same dress in different colours or different shades of the same colour? A popular style these days is a bodice and skirt ensemble as this gives them more option for future wear – the bodice top with a pair of black trousers would be perfect for a smart evening out.

At the end of the day all eyes will be on you, not them, but they should be there to complement and enhance your look – especially during the ceremony and in any photos when you will all be together. So don't decide on their dresses until you have chosen yours, and you know that you will all look good together as a group. A nice way to create a sense of unity is for the flowers in your bouquet to match their dresses or for them to wear matching flowers in their hair. Another nice touch is to find an accessory, perhaps a hair-clip, which matches your tiara. The bridesmaids dresses are also a good way of establishing or continuing any colour theme you have for your wedding.

Who wears what and how

So lots of options with the bridesmaids – be creative, but remember... be nice, this may be your day but they will also be on show and will want to look good too!

Where to shop

Most bridal shops stock different ranges of bridesmaids outfits. Popular ranges include the stunning Jim Hjelm Occasions collection (which includes a teenage range and a maternity range), and the modern and sassy Watters & Watters. However, as with everything else, it is worth checking out the high street shops such as Monsoon and Debenhams, or for a less formal and more modern look, try Oasis, Warehouse or Mango.

It is worth asking if one of your bridesmaids (or their mums!) can sew. Whilst most people are reluctant to make the wedding dress itself, bridesmaid dresses tend to be far more straightforward and doing this can save you a lot of money.

The Groom and Groomsmen

Men look damn sexy in kilts and I won't hear anyone say otherwise (and always at the back of your mind there is the naughty knowledge that they're wearing nothing underneath!)

So how do you wear it? Below is a rough guide for a man to dress himself in a kilt. I would thoroughly advise, however, that if you have never worn one before, you get help from the professionals.

The kilt

The kilt should be worn around the natural waistline (ie where your navel is) and should come to the centre of your knees (so that when you kneel it skims the ground). The pleats hang at the back of the kilt with the fringed edge to the right and the kilt pin approximately two inches in from the fringed edge and four inches up from the hem.

The sporran

The sporran is centred at the front of the kilt, approximately 6 inches from the top of the kilt. The chain passes through the loops on the back of the kilt and the strap fastens at the back.

Who wears what and how

The hose and flashes

The woollen kilt hose (socks) come to approximately two inches below the kneecap and are folded over at the top. The flashes are worn tucked under the fold of the sock, on the outside of the leg.

The sgian dubh

The sgian dubh (dagger – pronounced 'sgee n' doo') is normally worn down the right sock, although a left-handed person could wear it on the left leg. Only the top inch or two of the handle should show above the sock.

The ghillie brogues

These are the shoes most commonly worn with a kilt, with the laces tied up around the leg. To tie the laces on the Ghillie Brogue, cross the laces over each other three times and pull tight again to create a vertical thong along the shin. Pass the laces around the back of the calf and then bring to the front of the shin and tie a normal bow, with the laces and toggles hanging at the front.

Belt / Waistcoat

When wearing a waistcoat, no belt is worn and when wearing a belt, no waistcoat is worn.

The different styles

There are three different 'styles' of kilt wear: Daywear, Semi-formal (day/evening wear) and Evening wear.

Daywear includes all of the above plus a tweed jacket with matching five-button waistcoat, plain shirt and woollen tie. A leather sporran is commonly worn for daywear.

Semi-formal wear includes all of the above plus an Argyll jacket with matching five-button waistcoat, plain or dress shirt, either a woollen tie or bow tie and either a leather or formal sporran.

Evening wear includes all of the above plus the short black Prince Charlie jacket, matching three-button waistcoat, dress shirt and bow tie. The sporran worn for evening wear is made from fur

Who wears what and how

and/or is silver mounted. There is a Highland tradition of leaving the bottom button undone on the waistcoat – this is said to be done out of respect for Bonnie Prince Charlie whose expanded waistline meant that he could no longer do his up!

You will often see a mixture of all of the above styles worn at weddings. However, if you are planning on having your bridal party wearing kilts, you should ensure they all fit into one style, depending on the style of your wedding. It is not necessary for all the bridal party to wear the same tartan, as traditionally each person wears their own tartan according to their clan. If however you are hiring outfits for the entire bridal party, you may wish to co-ordinate tartans.

Alternatives

- **Trews** – if your groom/father can't quite see himself in a kilt, trews are becoming a popular alternative. They are particularly popular with the older generation, once the middle-aged spread has set in!

- **Plain Grey/Black Kilt** – as fashioned by Manchester's very own Robbie Williams! This is a very modern and versatile look, which can be teamed with a contemporary jacket or shirt.

- **Feileadh Mor/Breacan Feile** – classic Highlander look, made popular again by the film *Braveheart*. This one-piece kilt and plaid is often paired with a classic Jacobite (open-necked, laced) shirt.

- **Jacobean** – A more rugged and casual look. The kilt is worn with a Jacobite shirt and Potaine (sleeveless jacket).

Choosing your tartan

A person may wear any tartan of his or her choice except for tartans restricted by copyright or trademark and those reserved for members of the Royal Family (the Balmoral tartan). Generally you would wear the tartan of the clan that you belong to. If you cannot find a tartan that fits your surname, you may still be associated

Who wears what and how

with a clan. For example, if your surname is Adams, you are associated with the Gordon clan, or if your surname is Carson, you are associated with the MacPherson clan.

For those without a clan there are a number of district tartans that can be used, or the 'Hunting Stewart', which serves as the universal Scottish tartan. There are even tartans for non-Scots. For example, different regions of the UK have their own tartans, (there is a 'Tyneside' tartan and a 'Devon' tartan), different countries have their own tartans (there is an 'Australia' tartan) and if you are from the United States, there are a number of states that have their own, official or non-official, tartans with new ones being added every year.

A website where you can find your clan and corresponding tartan is www.clanshop.co.uk, and any kilt makers or hire shop will be able to advise on the right tartan for you.

Hire or buy?

To buy a full kilt outfit is expensive, and probably not worth doing unless you anticipate that it will be worn to future events, or unless you want a keepsake to go alongside the wedding dress. The obvious advantage of buying your outfit is that it will be made to measure and you will also have a greater choice of tartan and a greater choice of material, buttons etc. If buying, allow at least eight weeks for it to be made. Most Highland Dress shops also hire outfits, which is obviously a cheaper alternative. If you are hiring outfits for all the wedding party, check to see if they do any group discounts as is often the case. You can hire all the accessories too.

Do it *your* way

*Theming your event isn't about making it 'different',
it's about making it personal to you – a day for you
to remember because it was your day the way you
wanted it.*

Do it *your* way

Personalising your day

You will probably have an idea about how you see your wedding,
especially if, like most women, you have been planning this day
since you were a little girl (or at least since you met your man!).
So the first thing you need to do is to decide what kind of
wedding you want – religious or civil? Church, registration office or
other venue? Large or small? Formal or informal? Traditional or
contemporary?

Once you have sorted out a few of these things, you can turn
your focus to the theme of the wedding. When I say theme, I don't
necessarily mean turning your venue into an underwater world
and having your bridesmaids dressed as mermaids (well, whatever
floats your boat!) It is more a way of bringing together all the
aspects of the day and making them a whole. Whereas fifty years
ago the wedding day focused on the ceremony (or perhaps what the
bride looked like), more and more weddings today are about the
whole day – and more importantly the 'feel' of the whole day.
The wedding has become more than an official coming together of a
couple in love and more of a grand event.

So how do you choose your theme? As I have said, it doesn't need
to be a 'theme' as such. It can be more a suggestion of the time of
year you are marrying, or dictated by the venue in which you are
marrying, or perhaps a country where you met or a hobby which
brought the two of you together. Or perhaps you have a favourite
flower or colour or even a penchant for a certain type of food?
Or maybe you already have an idea in your head of how you
imagine your wedding day to be and can just elaborate on this.
If you can find something that is personal to you it will make the
day all the more special and memorable.

Imagine your day chronologically from when you arrive at the
ceremony (what transport will you arrive in?) to walking into the
ceremony venue (how will it be decorated? What music will be
playing? What will the readings be? What will the orders of service
look like? And what will you look like? what flowers will you be

Do it *your* way

carrying? What will the rest of the bridal party be wearing?) to the drinks reception (how will it be decorated? What music will be playing? What will people be drinking? and eating?) And on to the evening reception (how will it be decorated? What will people be eating and drinking? What will the tables look like? Will they be numbered or named? What table centres will there be? What about place settings? menus? name cards? favours? What will the cake look like? What entertainment will there be?). A well thought-out event can make a real impression and it is often the small, finishing touches that make all the difference.

Theming ideas

Medieval

Castle venue, scrolls as invitations, medieval dress, harpist playing during the drinks reception, candlelit medieval banquet with a hog roast for the wedding breakfast with long tables and goblets of wine, fighting clansmen as entertainment and a ceilidh to finish the night.

Christmas

Think greens, golds and reds – a candelit ceremony with carols, mulled wine, holly, ivy, mistletoe, candelit Christmas dinner, Christmas crackers for favours, a large Christmas tree and fairy lights to dress the room and fireworks to end the night with a bang!

Summer

Country house hotel or stately home, Pimms and lemonade with canapés or champagne and strawberries on the lawn, bright exotic flowers, swing jazz band, wedding breakfast in a marquee, dressed with flowers and butterflies, ice cream wedding cake served as dessert.

Modern oriental

Modern boutique hotel, jades and lilacs, bamboo and orchids, lychee martinis, modern Asian cuisine with chopsticks, fortune cookies as favours, and karaoke to finish the night.

Traditional Scottish

Castle venue, Celtic design stationery, Celtic wedding rings, highland dress, piper, haggis on the menu, whisky miniatures as favours, and a raucous ceilidh to end the night.

Even if you don't like the idea of a theme as such, ensuring that everything fits together will make a real difference to the feel of your wedding. For example, you can match the colour of the bridesmaids' dresses to the colour of the flowers in your bouquet to the flowers on the dinner tables, to the ribbon on the stationery... you get the picture.

It may sound obvious, but work with what you already have – trying to have a summer garden party in December clearly isn't going to work, just as a medieval theme won't work so well if you have already booked a modern boutique hotel as your venue.

Case Study

Marianne and Dougie, Christmas themed December wedding

Invitations

The invitations set the scene for the wedding – a modern Christmas design, featuring red ribbon of a colour, which would later be seen in the wedding flowers and bridesmaids' dresses.

Do it *your* way

Ceremony

Guests, dressed in black tie and evening dress, arrived for mulled wine and minced pies prior to the ceremony. The ceremony venue was candle lit and decorated with ivy and white and red roses. Christmas carols were sung in place of traditional hymns.

Drinks reception

Guests sipped champagne by open log fires with a CD of Frank Sinatra and Bing Crosby singing Christmas songs as background music. The venue was dressed for Christmas with a large Christmas tree in the foyer.

Reception

The room for the evening reception was decorated to reflect the theme of the day. A large Christmas tree highlighted one end of the room, with vases of twisted willow entwined with fairy lights lining the walls. Each table had ivy-covered candelabra as a centrepiece, with further tea lights on the tables offering the only other lighting. Gold and silver confetti and dried red rose petals further decorated the tables. The menus matched the invitations and order of service and the favours were filled silver and gold Christmas Crackers, which doubled as name cards. The wedding breakfast – Christmas dinner with a twist – ended with Christmas pudding ice cream. Having danced the night away, guests were treated to a fabulous firework display before being transported home.

Case Study

Susie and Mark, Traditional Scottish themed wedding

Invitations

The invitations set the scene for the wedding – a traditional Celtic design, inviting guests to a castle wedding just outside Inverness.

Do it *your* way

Ceremony

The guests were greeted by a piper at the doors to the castle.
The ceremony took place in the Old Keep of the castle, which was
decorated with flowers, including large thistles, echoing those in
the bride's and bridesmaids' bouquets. The piper then piped the
bride, dressed in a traditional white gown with a Celtic design
embroidered on the bodice, down the aisle to begin the ceremony.
Readings included Burns poetry, and background music for the
signing of the marriage schedule was traditionally Celtic.

Reception

All the tables for dinner were named after Scottish islands and had
thistle and flower centrepieces, matching the bouquets. The name
cards featured the Celtic design from the invitations and orders
of service, and tartan ribbons matching the groom's kilt replaced
conventional napkin rings. For the meal, guests ate haggis parcels,
scotch beef and traditional cranachan to finish. The guests were
given whisky miniatures for favours, and the night ended with a
lively ceilidh.

You are cordially invited...

Matching your invitations with your orders of service, your menus
and even your name cards for dinner is an effective way of carrying
the theme through the wedding and providing continuity.

Invitations

Your invitations are the first hint to your guests of the kind of day
they can expect, and are an ideal way of introducing your theme.
A traditional invitation on white card with calligraphy inside
indicates a formal wedding, whilst a card with a caricature of the
happy couple on the front will imply a less formal day. A coloured
ribbon can introduce your colour scheme, or parchment scrolls
could introduce a medieval theme. There are literally hundreds of
invitation suppliers out there offering all kinds of stationery from
the traditional to the trendy, or why not try your hand at making
your own? Be as creative as you dare!

Do it *your* way

Most major department stores have samples of wedding stationery from the main UK suppliers, or for more personalised stationery, look for companies in magazines or on the web who feature styles you like the look of. If you are ordering specially designed stationery, you should allow four to six months for it to be done, and always allow extra time in case of error. When ordering your stationery you may also want to consider ordering RSVP cards to include with the invitations, and thank you cards for later. Remember when ordering that you will only need one invitation per couple, and you should order a few spare in case of mistakes or for mementoes. If you are making your own invitations, you will need to ensure you can get suitable envelopes/packaging.

If you are getting married at a particularly popular time of year, it is becoming more common now to send 'Save the Date' cards – a way of letting those close to you know the date of your wedding before you are ready to finalise your list and write your invitations. 'Save the Date' magnets are popular too – this way your friends can stick it to their fridge, so they are sure not to forget!

For more formal invitations, you may want to hire a calligrapher who can add the finishing touches to your elegant stationery to help make a good impression. For less formal invitations this may not be necessary, but you should still ensure they are written by someone with nice handwriting and with a nice pen. A spidery scrawl will ruin the effect of a classy invitation!

Wording for invitations is generally fairly formal and there is much etiquette surrounding this. A few examples are shown below. However, as with everything, you should feel free to re-word this to suit yourselves, your family (divorced parents, widowed mother etc.) and your wedding. Just make sure you include the names of the hosts and the bride and groom, the date and time, the venue, and an RSVP address.

Parents of the bride as host:

Mr & Mrs James Sinclair

Request the pleasure of the company of

. . . .

at the marriage of their daughter

Suzanne Jane

with

Mr David Lee McDonald

at Greyfriars Kirk, Edinburgh

on Saturday 16th August 2007

at three o'clock

and afterwards at

Norton House Hotel

17 Mount Close   R.S.V.P by
Inverness IV4 4DN   1st July 2007

Bride and groom as hosts

Suzanne Sinclair and David McDonald

Request the company of

. . . .

at their marriage

at Greyfriars Kirk, Edinburgh

on Saturday 16th August 2007

at three o'clock

The reception afterwards will be held at

Norton House Hotel

Please reply to:

24 St Patricks Place
Edinburgh EH2 4SE
By 1st July 2007

Do it *your* way

Parents of bride as host – evening

Mr & Mrs James Sinclair
would like you to join them
at Norton House Hotel, Edinburgh
on Saturday 16th August 2007
from eight o'clock
to celebrate the marriage of their daughter
Suzanne Jane
with
Mr David Lee McDonald

Please reply to:
17 Mount Close, Inverness, IV4 4DN   By 1st July 2007

Bride and groom as hosts – evening

Suzanne Sinclair and David McDonald
request the pleasure of the company of

. . . .

at a Wedding Dance to be held at
Norton House Hotel, Edinburgh
on Saturday 16th August 2007
from eight o'clock

Please reply to:
24 St Patricks Place, Edinburgh
EH2 4SE   By 1st July 2007

There may be additional information you may want to include
on your invitations. For example you may have specific dress
requirements – 'Black Tie', 'Evening Dress', 'Medieval Dress',
'No Jeans' etc. Or you may wish to include a finishing time – more
formally this can be written as 'Carriages at Midnight' (if transport
is provided). Another useful line to add is 'Please advise of any
dietary requirements in your reply'.

If you are including children on the invitation, it is polite to use the children's names rather than '...and family'. If you are not inviting children, it may be wise to include a tactful phrase such as 'We regret that we cannot accommodate children' to avoid any embarrassing explanations to individual friends or worse yet, unexpected guests on the day!

Top Tip

Put a note in with your invitations saying that there will be a prize for the first person to reply, and watch those replies come flying through your letterbox!

What else should be included in the envelope?

You should include maps and directions to the ceremony and reception venues, and any car parking information, if necessary. If you have guests travelling for your wedding it is normal to include a list of nearby hotels and/or guests houses and their prices, and you may also want to include some local tourist information for them. If you are providing transport, either to the venue, or at the end of the night, you should include information about this also, and ask for people to let you know if this will be required so that you can get an idea of numbers when you come to book it. You may also wish to include details of your gift list if you are having one. Another finishing touch is to include a handful of confetti so that it falls out when your guests open the envelope, to get them in the wedding spirit! An A-Z is a popular way of compiling all this information into a document – an example one is shown below.

Example A–Z

Arrival

Please can guests ensure they have arrived and are seated in the church by 12.45pm.

Bar

Please note that the venue has a cash only bar for the reception.

Do it *your* way

Confetti

Biodegradable confetti or rose petals are allowed at the church.

Dancing

We have a band booked for the evening reception so please bring your dancing shoes!

Etiquette

Etiquette traditionally asks you to wait for the bride and groom to depart before you do. We intend on staying at the reception until the end, so please feel free to leave when you are ready.

Food

Please let us know in advance if you have any food allergies or special dietary requirements so we can inform the hotel and offer alternatives.

Gifts

We have a gift list at www.honeymoney.co.uk. Please do not feel obliged to buy us anything as this is only intended as a guide to those who want to use it.

Honeymoon

We have planned a honeymoon to remember in Dubai and the Maldives. Please see our gift list (above) for more information.

Instant Camera

We will be taking your photo with an instant camera – please can you stick your photo in the guest book with your message.

Jokes

John Smith will be the best man and we have no doubt that he will keep us entertained during his speech (no pressure!).

Kisses

Please feel free to kiss the bride, but remember she will be a married woman so nothing rude!

Do it *your* way

Lost

We don't want you to get lost on your way, so please use the directions we have included!

Mobile phones

Please ensure that all phones are switched off during the ceremony and speeches.

No Smoking

Please note that it is a non-smoking venue.

Official photos

Official photos will be taken between the ceremony and reception. Your presence is requested in front of the venue at 3:30pm for the group shot.

Parking

There is parking available at the venue.

Questions

If you have any questions please give us a call.

RSVP

Please RSVP by 3rd June. There will be a prize for the first RSVP we receive!

Signing

A guest book will be passed around the reception, please sign it and leave us a message.

Transport

A coach will leave from the train station at 1pm and will return at midnight.

Ushers

Our ushers will be on hand throughout the day to answer any queries and show you where to go.

Do it *your* way

Videographer

There will be a videographer filming throughout – please do your best to act normally!

Website

For further information and links to the venue have a look at www...

Xtra info

If there is anything else that you wish to know then please get in touch.

Young Guests

There will be a bouncy castle and in the grounds for the younger guests (or young at heart!)

Zzz

We have a special rate with the hotel for guests. Please use our names as a booking reference.

Orders of service

An order of service, or an order of ceremony for a civil wedding, will show your guests what will happen and in what order, and in the case of a church wedding avoids the need to juggle service book, hymn book etc. As well as detailing music, hymns and readings, it gives you the opportunity to name readers and musicians, or soloists. It is normal to include all the words to any hymns sung, whilst readings can be introduced merely by the title or first line. If you are having a religious ceremony, be sure to get the minister's approval and ensure his or her name is correct before having your orders of service printed.

The following is an example of a standard order of service. Obviously each ceremony is individual and the order of service will reflect this.

Do it *your* way

front page	inside
St Michaels Church	Entrance music for bride
Cupar	Introduction
	Hymn – written in full
The marriage of	The marriage (Minister's name)
Maria Douglas	Readings – title only (optional)
&	Prayers – title only (optional)
Steven Mackenzie	Hymn – written in full
	Reading/blessing – title only (optional)
Saturday 26th July 2003	Signing of the wedding schedule
	(Musical interlude – title/musicians)
	Retiral music

Many modern weddings now include an order of the day, detailing timings of the drinks reception, group photos, wedding breakfast etc. This is a good way of ensuring all your guests know what is going on, especially when weddings are becoming more and more varied.

Copyright

You may need to pay copyright to reproduce the hymns in your order of service. Copyright exists in creative works such as hymns for 70 years after the death of the writer. During that period, it is illegal to reproduce the work in any form without the permission of the copyright holder. You will find details of the copyright holder at the bottom of the page in a hymnbook.

A charge of between £10 and £25 is usually made (although many of the hymns are out of copyright due to their age). Check with your stationery providers as they may take care of the copyright issue on your behalf.

If you do not intend to reprint the words and decide to use hymn-books instead, you will not need the copyright holder's permission.

Flower power

Flowers can play a huge part in theming your wedding, and are an easy way of tying everything in together. Merely matching

Do it *your* way

some flowers from your bouquet to those in the arrangements in the ceremony venue to those on your banqueting tables is an easy and effective way of bringing together the different parts of your day. Matching the colours of your flowers to the bridesmaids' dresses or the ribbons on your stationery/favours etc. is another way to show your wedding to be a well thought-out event. Brides are becoming more adventurous when it comes to choosing their flowers and decorations, so have some fun and be creative!

Choosing a florist

Personal recommendations are a good way to find a florist. If you don't have any recommendations, you will need to keep your eyes open. Have a look in florists' shop windows as you are out shopping or as you pass in the bus on your way to work – you will be able to get a good idea of their style by the type of flowers and displays they have in their windows. If you see a display you particularly like in a bar, restaurant or office, ask them who does their flowers. Or all else failing, look in the Yellow Pages. Make a short list of ones that catch your eye and go and see them. I would recommend going to see at least three different florists – if for nothing else, to get an idea of reasonable costs, and even if you don't use them, you may be able to use some of their ideas!

Look through their portfolios – look for similar styles to what you are considering (ie. modern, traditional, wacky, tropical, oriental etc), and look to see if they have any examples of work they have done either in your venue or in similar venues. It will help to take along swatches of material from both your dress and the bridesmaids' dresses, and if possible photos of the dresses, to help the florist to match flowers and design complementary bouquets and decorations.

Ask the florist for advice and listen to their suggestions – you will want someone who is going to get excited about the different types of flowers you could have, rather than see it as 'another wedding'. If you have a budget in mind, let the florist know so they can help you achieve the best look for your budget. Most importantly though, make sure they share your vision and understand what you want to achieve… and don't let them talk you into having pineapples and artichokes as your centrepieces if they just aren't your thing!

What will you need?

Obviously you will need a bouquet – but what about all the other things you might not have considered? You will also need some or all of the following: bouquets for your bridesmaids, posies or baskets for the flower girls, hair decorations for yourself or the bridesmaids, buttonholes for the men in the bridal party, corsages for the mothers, decorations for the ceremony venue, decorations for the reception venue, flowers for the cake or cake table, table centres for the banqueting tables and thank you bouquets for the mothers. Ideally you should aim to ensure all of these tie in together or complement each other in some way.

Bouquets

You will need a bouquet for both yourself and the bridesmaids. The bridesmaids' bouquets are usually smaller versions of the bride's bouquet – or are at least designed to complement the bride's bouquet. Again, flower girls carry smaller versions of the bride's bouquet or, if they are very young, it may be easier for them to carry a basket. Another alternative is to give the flower girl a basket of petals, which she could scatter in your path as you walk up the aisle. There are many different styles of bouquet, from a hand-tied posy of wild flowers to a tumbling cascade of tropical blooms – your florist will be able to advise you on what will best suit your dress, theme and budget. Think of your bouquet as the final touch to your wedding dress and choose it with this in mind.

Buttonholes/corsages

Buttonholes are worn by the men in the bridal party – usually the groom, best man, father of the bride and ushers. Corsages are worn by the two mothers. Mothers who don't want to ruin their outfits by pinning on their corsages can opt to pin it to their bag or can wear it round their wrist on elastic. You can also get fixings that

Do it *your* way

use magnets instead of pins, but make sure the flowers you choose aren't too heavy, as they don't take much weight! Other family members may also like to wear a buttonhole or corsage, so it is best to check with them before you order your flowers. Usually button-holes and corsages are made up of a single flower, matching those in the bride's bouquet – traditional Scottish buttonholes use either thistles or heather (which is considered to be lucky). Whatever you decide, be careful to choose flowers that last well, so they don't wilt half-way through the day.

Hair decorations

Depending on how traditional or contemporary you want to be, there are endless possibilities with what you can do here. A very traditional look, which may suit a summer country wedding or medieval themed wedding, is to wear a wreath of flowers. Alternatively, a single striking flower pinned in your hair or little rosebuds dotted amongst an up-do are both very pretty, modern looks.

Ceremony and venue decorations

Usually there are one or two pedestals of flowers or large displays at the front of the church or ceremony venue, to carry the theme into the room. Depending on the venue, you may feel this is enough to theme the room. Popular additions however are flowers for the ends of the pews, window ledges, or entrances.

In the reception venue, again this will depend on the style of the venue and your budget. You may choose to go flower mad and line your marquee with a flower-filled trellis, or you may prefer a few carefully placed displays – remember less is often more, especially if you are going for a contemporary look. Areas to look out for which may lend themselves to being floral display areas are mantelpieces, window ledges, pillars, entrance halls, table centres (more on these later) and corners of the room. Visit the venue with your florist if possible and try to envisage how you want it to look and think about the ambience you want to create as you walk into each room.

Depending on the logistics of your wedding, you may be able to double up your decorations and move them from the ceremony to the reception venue.

Ten things your florist will need to know

- **When is your wedding?**
  Summer or winter? Morning or evening?

- **What is the theme of your wedding?**
  Any particular theme that will affect the flowers you may choose, eg. Oriental, tropical, Christmas etc.

- **What atmosphere are you trying to create/what impression do you want to give?**
  Formal or informal? Grand and ostentatious or subtle and stylish? Traditional or contemporary? Romantic and moody? Fun and flirty?

- **Do you have any particular colours in mind?**
  Take swatches of material from the dresses, any ribbon being used, samples of your stationery – anything that has a particular colour you want carried through to your flowers.

- **What is your dress like? Shape? Colour? Accessories?**
  If possible take a picture of it, and a swatch of material. Your florist will need to have a good idea of how you will look in order to design a bouquet to show it off to best effect.

- **What will everybody else be wearing? Colours? Accessories?**
  This will help the florist design the bridesmaids' bouquets and buttonholes for the groomsmen and may also affect other displays.

- **Are there any particular must-haves?**
  If you envisage having orchids or you love white roses, let your florist know.

- **Are there any particular must not-haves?**
  If you hate carnations or are allergic to lilies – again be sure to let your florist know.

Do it *your* way

- **How will you be wearing your hair?**
  Up or down? Will you be wearing a tiara, veil, hair-clips?

- **What is your budget?**
  Giving your florist an idea of your budget will allow them to provide a realistic idea of what they can achieve.

Money matters and cost saving

- Generally speaking, greenery is cheaper than flowers – so to save money, use greenery to bulk out the displays, with flowers being used sparingly.

- Dried plants such as twisted willow branches can be used to create very modern displays. They are also a more cost-effective way of forming displays as florists can re-use them.

- Using a single, striking flower in place of a bouquet can be a modern, yet cheap alternative to either the bride or bridesmaids' bouquets. Finish it with a trailing ribbon in satin or organza.

- Similarly, using a single or pair of striking flowers can make a modern and chic table centre.

- Double up – if practical, think of moving your displays to the reception venue once the ceremony is over.

- Go for in-season and locally grown flowers – your florist will be able to advise on this.

- Go halves – if you are getting married in a church or other venue where there may be more than one wedding on the same day, it may be worth getting in touch with the other bride to see if you can share the cost of your flowers.

- If you are having a long top table, you could use your bouquet as the table decoration. Or you could use it to decorate the cake table.

Have your cake and eat it

A beautiful cake can be the *pièce de résistance* for your wedding. It is amazing what cake decorators can do with sugar crafting and the like. Choose a few cake decorators out of the Yellow Pages and if possible go and have a look in the shop window or at their portfolio to get an idea of the quality of their decorating. However, you will need to be prepared to pay the price if you want anything very elaborate or out of the ordinary.

Traditionally a wedding cake is a fruitcake with marzipan and white icing. These days however brides are opting for chocolate sponges, carrot cakes, or whatever happens to be their favourite flavour! If you want to follow the tradition of freezing the top tier for your first baby's christening however, you will need to ensure that the top tier at least is a fruitcake, as it is the only type suitable for this. Likewise if you are planning on sending slices of cake to people who were unable to attend the wedding, fruitcake is the best choice as it keeps a long time.

A traditional tiered cake is still a popular choice, but increasingly so are all manner of different designs. Recently I have seen cakes that resembled the castle in which the wedding was taking place, the car in which the bride arrived, and even the couple's pet dog! The traditional figurines of the bride and groom on top of the cake are now being replaced with caricature models of the bride and groom, flowers or even sparklers.

If you are trying to keep your budget down, the cake is an easy place to save money. Most people can find a friend or relative who can make cakes, or Marks and Spencer do very reasonable, good cakes with plain white icing. You can either have this decorated or simply ask your florist to include some flowers for the top. Look in cake decorating shops for coloured ribbon, sparklers or other decorations you could add yourself.

If you want to be more adventurous, how about an ice cream cake or a tiered pavlova for a summer wedding? Or a Croquembouche (profiterole tower) to make a real impression? Individual fairy cakes piled into tiers are also becoming a popular choice. Look for inspiration in magazines for cakes that may suit your wedding ideas.

Do it *your* way

Do me a favour!

Favours are a fun way of reflecting your theme and giving your guests a little memento of it to take away with them. The tradition of giving guests keepsakes or thank you gifts has been around for hundreds of years, and is a tradition that we have adopted from Italy, where the traditional gift was five sugared almonds (five being a number which cannot be divided, like the bride and groom), which represented health, wealth, happiness, fertility and long life. According to Scottish tradition, favours were given to 12 ladies of the party.

Today, however, favours are normally presented to all female guests at the wedding, and sometimes to the males too. Sugared almonds have now given way to just about anything you can imagine, and favours have become a popular way to express your individuality. There are hundreds of favour companies out there who will provide you with anything you want from organza bags filled with chocolates, to engraved wine glasses, to miniature flower pots, to… you name it.

They needn't cost you a lot of money either, and if you are trying to keep your budget down, favours are one of the easiest details of your wedding to make yourself, and get friends, family, or brides-maids involved in. A simple method is to buy a length of tulle or organza from a fabric shop, cut to size, fill with your gift and finish with a ribbon to match your colour scheme. Any favour company will also be able to provide you with bags or boxes in any shape, colour and material which you can fill with sweets of your choice – jelly beans, Love Hearts, Scottish tablet, chocolate mints etc.
Au Naturale are a good source of cheap candles and little gifts, which would make great favours. Or try Boots or The Body Shop for miniature soaps/shower gels etc. You can also double up the favours with name cards for the meal setting, which could also help save on costs. If you don't want to give out favours individually, you could fill bowls with sweets and put them on the tables for people to share – flying saucers in glass bowls are particularly effective.

Do it *your* way

Ideas for favours

- Organza bags filled with forget-me-not seeds
- Miniature packets of 'just married' Love Heart sweets
- Single red roses/thistles/gerbera (to tie in with the wedding flowers)
- Personalised napkin rings with the date of the wedding (can double as place settings)
- Miniatures of whisky (or Baileys, or any other liqueur) with or without personalised labels
- Matchbooks with your names and the date of the wedding
- Personalised champagne glasses – these can be used for the toasts then taken away
- Lottery tickets – rolled up and tied with a ribbon to match your colour scheme
- Scented candles
- Lollipops or sticks of rock – these can be personalised and wrapped with a coloured ribbon
- Fortune cookies
- Photo frames
- Bubbles – these come in all kinds of shapes now, including champagne bottles and wedding cakes
- Miniature shower gels/body lotions/perfumes wrapped in tulle and finished with a ribbon
- Wedding crackers – these can be ordered to match your colour scheme and can either be filled for you or left open for you to add your own gift
- CDs with music tracks from your wedding
- Paper fans – for an oriental themed or summer wedding

Most of the above are fairly general and could be used at any wedding. However, if you can, It is nice to think of something that is really 'you' or that really ties in with your wedding, as this will serve as more of a reminder of your day for your guests.

Do it *your* way

Party time!

Your reception venue is where your guests will end up and spend most of the day, so it is an ideal opportunity to add all those finishing little touches that people will have the time to notice. Think of the room as a whole, and of the banqueting tables themselves as this is where people will be sitting.

Lighting

The effect of lighting in setting the atmosphere of a room should be underestimated. When you visit your venue, play around with the room lighting – most venues have dimmable lighting and separate channels. Avoid using the fluorescent lights at all costs – they do no favours to anyone! Candlelight is fantastic for not only establishing a romantic mood but also provides a flattering light, and will provide that 'special occasion' ambience. Whether you go for tall dramatic candelabra, a floating candle arrangement, or many small tea lights dotted about will depend on the image you are trying to create… the possibilities are, of course, endless. Fairy lights also add a romantic touch – these can be incorporated into your room décor or floral arrangements. If you have the budget, consider hiring a lighting company who will be able to give experienced advice and suggestions and provide the lighting to really alter the image of the room.

Table centres

Table centres are another fun way of carrying through your theme, and again the possibilities are limited only by your imagination. One point to bear in mind however is that you don't want them to obstruct your guests' view of each other – so they need to either be high or low, or transparent. A popular choice is a tall candelabrum, finished with flowers to match the bouquets etc, as is a simple, low floral arrangement, often combined with candles. More modern arrangements often include twisted willow (remember this can be spray painted any colour), vases filled with coloured water or gel to enhance your colour theme, goldfish bowls filled with flowers, and ice sculptures, which can come in any shape or size you wish.

Do it *your* way

The tables

You don't want to clutter the tables – remember you will need room for crockery, cutlery and glasses. (These themselves can be sourced specially to complement your theme, using different styles and colours of glass, china or underplates.) However, there are many additional finishing touches you may like to add:

Coloured tablecloths and matching chair covers can make a big difference to the overall look of the room. These come in a wealth of different colours, patterns and materials, with organza being particularly appropriate for weddings. Your caterer should be able to source these for you or, if not, there are companies who specialise in linen hire.

Table confetti is a fun way of continuing the 'wedding' feel of your day and there is an amazing variety of colours, shapes and themes – hearts, stars, 'just married' shapes, reindeer… and tartan confetti is now available too! Or perhaps real petal confetti will be more appropriate to your theme – again coming in different colours and types of flower, but take care to ensure it is non-staining or you could find yourself facing a rather large dry cleaning bill!

Wedding crackers can double as favours and name place cards and are a good way of breaking the ice amongst your guests as they have to pull them with their neighbour and you can include a joke or tongue twister to get the fun started.

Disposable cameras are a popular addition to the tables, allowing for plenty of informal shots of the fun part of the day.

Menus and name place cards can either be printed to match the other wedding stationery, or why not be more inventive? It is often possible to double up your favours with your place cards, simply by labelling each one. Other options could be individually iced cakes or cookies, or perhaps pebbles with names written on for a beach themed wedding, named baubles for a Christmas wedding, or individualised leaves for an autumnal wedding. Alternatively you could use funky name cardholders to jazz up plainer name cards.

Picture perfect

Take time selecting your photographer, and allow as much money as you can afford to get a good one. Remember that your photographs will hold your memories of your big day and you cannot go back and re-shoot them once it is all over.

Picture perfect

Which style?

Every photographer, like every artist, has his or her own style of photography. You should really take the time to shop around and find a style you feel will work for you. These days the majority of photographers shoot on digital format and have websites displaying examples of their work. This is a quick and easy way to look at several different companies and form a shortlist of photographers you like. You can then order brochures from your shortlisted companies to help you further narrow down your choices.

Although every photographer has his or her own individual style, there are some general styles of wedding photography, and you will probably already have an idea of which will suit you.

Traditional photographers will work through a comprehensive list of posed shots designed to show the bride and groom, and their guests, off to their best. Traditional photographers will position you at the correct angle, show you how to stand, and will take the time to ensure the background, lighting and framing of each shot is just right, to achieve the best image possible.

Reportage photography is becoming more popular today as many couples are choosing to move away from the formality of the traditional style, and are instead opting for a means of recording the day as it unfolds from beginning to end, conveying the overall feel of the wedding. This style of photography tends to focus less predominantly on the bride and groom and will take in the guests and details such as the flower decorations, the stationery, the outfits etc. A good reportage photographer will capture those unique moments – a certain look between the bride and groom, the bride's mother's tears, the guests laughing over a glass of champagne – which make each wedding special. For this reason, reportage photography tends to be more expensive as the photographer will go through more film and will have to work that bit harder to be in the right place at the right time.

Avant-garde photography is a more artistic, abstract style, which you may wish to incorporate into your pictures, if you can find the

Picture perfect

right photographer. An example of an Avant-garde photograph would be one in which the subject (ie. the bride and groom) is not the focus of the shot – there may be a candlestick in the foreground with the bride and groom silhouetted against the church entrance in the background – thereby conveying the mood of the scene without actually focusing on the couple at all. It is unlikely that you will want all of your photographs to be in this style, but a few could really enhance your album and give it that 'Wow!' factor you are looking for.

Choosing your photographer

Once you have shortlisted a few photographers whose style and budget suit you, make appointments to go and visit them. Have a look at their portfolios, and more importantly, ask to see sample albums of other people's weddings. This is vital as it gives you the opportunity to see the final, complete product, rather than a carefully chosen selection in a portfolio.

Secondly, ensure you spend time talking to the photographer. (It is especially important if you are dealing with a larger company with several photographers on their books to ensure you meet the person who will be doing your wedding.) You and your guests will be spending a lot of time with your photographer on your wedding day and you will want to know that he or she will not offend anyone or drive you round the bend! Ask as many questions as you like (see box below for sample questions to ask) and make sure you feel comfortable spending time with him or her. This is also a good opportunity to plug photographers for ideas – remember that they attend hundreds of weddings a year and will have a good idea of what works and what doesn't.

Once you have found your perfect photographer – make a booking! Good photographers get booked up well in advance and you don't want to miss out.

Picture perfect

Questions to ask… your shortlisted photographers

What is included in the various packages?

Can I keep a copy of all the proofs? (Many packages include a number of prints, eg. 30 prints, which you choose from the proofs. Reportage photographers tend to include a copy of all the proofs in the package in addition to the enlarged 30 prints, as it is the proofs which tell the story of the day. With traditional photographers you may need to make special arrangements to keep the proofs.)

Do you work alone or with a partner?

What do you wear on the day?

Is travel to the venue included in the cost?

Who is responsible for food and refreshments?

Putting together your shot list

Nearer your wedding day you will need to meet with your photographer to finalise your requirements. Before you go, make a provisional list of all the shots you want. (An example list is shown below.) Once at the photographer's studio, have another look through the portfolio and example albums (particularly look to see if they have any from your venue) and point out any shots or styles you especially like – and anything you really don't like. By the time you leave you should have agreed your final shot list for the big day.

Top Tip

On the day you should assign somebody – usually an usher – to act as the photographer's assistant to help identify and round up the correct people for each shot. Make sure he also has a copy of your shot list. This will save a lot of time on the day, ultimately giving you more time to mingle with your guests.

Picture perfect

Most photographers now provide prints in a variety of colour, black and white and sepia and many also offer digital colour enhancement and hand tinting (for example, a black and white photograph of the bride and groom with just the confetti in colour). Now is the time to clarify which you would like.

You should also give your photographer a copy of the schedule for your day so that all movements can be anticipated and finally double-check he or she is due to arrive at the time and place you are expecting!

A note on copyright:

Normally the photographer owns copyright on the photographs he or she takes. This means you are not permitted to reproduce them in any way without permission – this includes putting them onto websites or copying them onto a CD. *Unless you make special arrangements to buy the negatives, all additional prints will need to be bought through the photographer.*

Example shot list

The list below is to help you consider different photos so that you can create your own shot list. Your photographer will be able to advise on a realistic number of shots in your timescale – or a realistic timescale for the number of shots you want. He or she will also have plenty of ideas of different poses for the bride and groom together. Even if you are going for reportage style photography there may be a few shots that you will want to make sure your photographer captures.

Picture perfect

Getting ready:

Groom and best man getting ready (to include tying bow ties etc)

Bride and bridesmaids getting ready (to include hair, nails, makeup etc)

Prior to ceremony:

Bride alone

Bride with bridesmaids

Bride's mother with bridesmaids

Bride and father leaving the house

Bride arriving at the church/venue

Bride close up through veil

Groom alone

Groom and best man outside church/venue

Groom with ushers

Outdoor shot of church/venue

Ceremony:

Bride and father walking down aisle

Bride and groom exchanging vows

Bride and groom exchanging rings

Bride and groom signing marriage schedule

Bride and groom with minister

First kiss

View from back of church, to include congregation

Procession leaving the church/venue

After the ceremony:

Bride and groom

Bride and groom with wedding party

Bride and groom with bride's family

Bride and groom with groom's family

Bride with her parents

Groom with his parents

Bride/groom with siblings

Bride/groom with grandparents

Bride and groom with flower girl/page boy

Bride with all the men in kilts

Child handing horseshoe to bride

Bride and groom with piper

Guests throwing confetti

All guests

Bride and groom leaving in car (inside and outside car)

Picture perfect

Informal group shots at drinks reception:

Bride or groom with school/college friends

Members of hen/stag parties

Reception:

Receiving line

Cutting the cake

Speeches and toasts

First dance

Tossing the bouquet

Detail shots to include:

Close up of dress detail

Shoes

Flowers

Rings

Stationery – orders of service/menus

Cake

Venue decorations

Table decorations

Candles

Favours

Videography

Many couples today are choosing to have a videographer in addition to a photographer as they feel a video can convey the overall atmosphere of the day, particularly if they opt for more formal photographs. Video can obviously record sound so the sound of the piper, the laughter of your guests, the popping of champagne corks, the moving and amusing words of the best man's speech and the music from your first dance will all be captured. Although often a substantial cost, it is something that, if they opt against it, many brides regret not having.

As with photographers, all videographers have their own style and you will need to find one that suits you. Look through the *Scottish Wedding Directory*, the Yellow Pages and on the internet, or ask friends or your photographer for recommendations and create your shortlist. Ask if they have sample videos for you to view – and ask to see a complete video of a couple's wedding in addition to a showreel so that you know what to expect in the finished product.

Only you will know what kind of video you are looking for – do you like slow-mo and soft focus or are you looking for something more contemporary? Consider also if you just want the ceremony

Picture perfect

filming, or do you want someone there from when you are getting ready right through to the dancing at night? Do you want it to include interviews with the bridal party and guests, or do you just want the whole programme cut to a music track?

Check what is included – how long the final programme will be and whether you can make any changes within the cost you have been quoted. Also, what music it will be set to, and whether you can choose this. Check how many copies are included in the price and how much it will be for further copies to be made. Also ask whether the videographer can provide the final programme on DVD as opposed to VHS – most companies do this now and the quality will be much better.

If you really can't, or won't, justify the additional cost of paying for a professional video to be made (a good wedding video will cost you upwards of £600), you could consider asking a friend or relative to stand in. Remember though that producing a video is something that requires skill and talent and a home video will generally look like just that. Having said that, many people now have editing software on their home computers, and their own camcorders, which they are used to using, and you may prefer the personal touch that it produces. A friend or relative will know you better and is likely to know several of your guests also, so people may feel more comfortable in front of them too. Just don't expect a Hollywood blockbuster if you do decide to go down this route!

Get me to the church on time

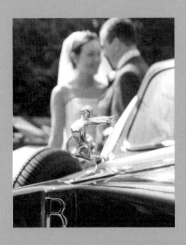

For many brides it is the moment when they are sitting in the car on the way to the ceremony that it really sinks in – 'I'm getting married!' Make sure you really mark this momentous occasion and choose transport that will get you there in style.

Get me to the church on time

What's your style?

As with the other aspects of your wedding it is a good idea to tie in your transport to the theme of your wedding – the overall feel of a medieval wedding will be ruined if the bride arrives in a stretch limo! The bride arriving on horseback however could really enhance the theme of the day and will guarantee a grand entrance and fantastic photo opportunities. Think also of the colour you choose – white is the traditional colour for a wedding car, but who needs to be traditional? You could choose the colour to continue the colour theme of your wedding, but remember that you are likely to have your photo taken with the car and so it should not clash with your dress. In the same way, a white or ivory dress will stand out better against a darker coloured car than a white one.

Horse and carriage

For the ultimate in traditional romance, you can't beat arriving in a horse and carriage. However, bear in mind the obvious drawbacks too – it is a slow mode of transport, and so trying to cover long distances is out (although you could always meet it halfway), and going up steep hills are also a no-go area. If you opt for an open carriage, make sure there is some way of covering it in case of rain, and ensure you see this prior to the day. There will normally be plenty of room for a large dress, but keep your dress and train away from the wheels and undercarriage which are likely to be muddy.

Vintage car

A beautiful vintage car remains the most popular mode of wedding transport as it offers a traditional and classy way of arriving for your big day, with just the right amount of pomp and stateliness to make you feel special, without the drama of a horse and carriage. There are several companies throughout Scotland offering wedding car hire with a wide range of makes and models to choose from. They tend to frequent the wedding fairs so you can have a good look at all the different cars there.

Get me to the church on time

Stretch limo

A more modern option, a stretch limo can provide you with the 'superstar' entrance you deserve on your wedding day, and is particularly suited to a more contemporary wedding. They are hugely spacious inside, so you can travel to the ceremony with all your bridesmaids and parents, and the groom can fit all his ushers in – providing a fun way to start the day. Offering all mod cons, you can provide a CD for your choice in drive time entertainment, and will have a fridge for chilling your champagne (check to see if the champagne is complimentary as part of the package).

Do check the doors prior to hiring – stretch limo doors tend to be quite narrow and if you have a large dress this could cause you problems. It is worth asking however, as some cars come with an additional 'bridal door' which is larger, to allow for a more dignified exit! Another point to note is that although some cars may be able to seat up to 14 people, by law they are only permitted to carry eight passengers plus the driver.

Supercar

Perhaps you or your loved one have always dreamt of a spin in a Ferrari 360 Modena or an Aston Martin DB9? (There aren't many men who haven't!) Hell, it's your wedding day – why not?! Go for it… isn't today all about living out your fantasies? There are even companies who will provide a James Bond look-alike chauffeur!

'I felt very conscious that our wedding day was very much about creating the day that I had imagined, so I wanted to do something for Pete that would help make it his dream day too. I hired a Porsche 911 and arranged for it to be delivered to the house for him to drive to the church in. He thought I was the best bride ever!'

Tanya

Get me to the church on time

Something more unusual?

Provided your venue has the facility, you could fly in and out on a helicopter for a true movie star entrance, and combine it with a fantastic sightseeing trip. Or how about sharing a bottle of champagne on a hot air balloon between the ceremony and the reception? Time it to coincide with sunset and you could not get more romantic. Or perhaps your dream is to arrive in a New York cab, a fire engine, or on the back of a Harley Davidson? If you don't know someone who can help you with the truly unusual, the Internet is probably your best bet... Keep searching – where there's a will, there's a way!

Car etiquette

The number of cars you need will depend on how far you have to travel (if it isn't far you can often use the same car to make two trips, especially as you often pay a minimum hire charge of three hours anyway), and how large your wedding party is. Traditionally, three cars are used:

Car 1 takes the bride and her father to the ceremony, then the newlyweds to the reception.

Car 2 takes the bridesmaids and the bride's mother to the ceremony, then the best man and bridesmaids to the reception.

Car 3 takes the groom and best man to the ceremony, then the bride and groom's parents to the reception.

Get me to the church on time

Top Tips

- Make sure there is room in the car for your dress – you don't want to arrive all crumpled!

- Ensure you will be getting the exact car you have seen, and not just a similar one.

- Check the contract regarding the right to substitute vehicles.

- Ask whether the cost includes ribbon on the front of the car and flowers on the back shelf.

- Ensure it will be thoroughly cleaned (inside and out) and polished before coming to collect you.

- Check whether you are allowed to drink in the car (a glass of champagne will help calm your nerves on the way to the ceremony!)

- If you are going for a convertible, ensure you have seen the car with the roof both up and down.

Guests

If your ceremony is far from the reception venue, or the wedding is going to be based out of town, or you have a lot of people flying in for the wedding, it is a nice gesture to provide your guests with transport. This will also mean you have less people driving and they are therefore more likely to let their hair down and have a good time!

Let your guests know in your invitations that you will be providing a coach leaving from an easy-to-get-to central point which will take guests to the ceremony, from the ceremony to the reception, and then return them to the central point after the reception. Ask them to let you know in their reply whether they will require this transport and then you will have numbers for booking. It is a good idea to provide another coach for additional evening guests also. It does take a bit of organising and co-ordination but your guests will really appreciate it. You can put one of your ushers on transport duty on the day so that you don't need to worry about it.

Eat, drink and be merry

The reception is the part of the day that most of your guests will look forward to. Weddings today have become less formal and more about having a great party – so make sure yours is one to remember!

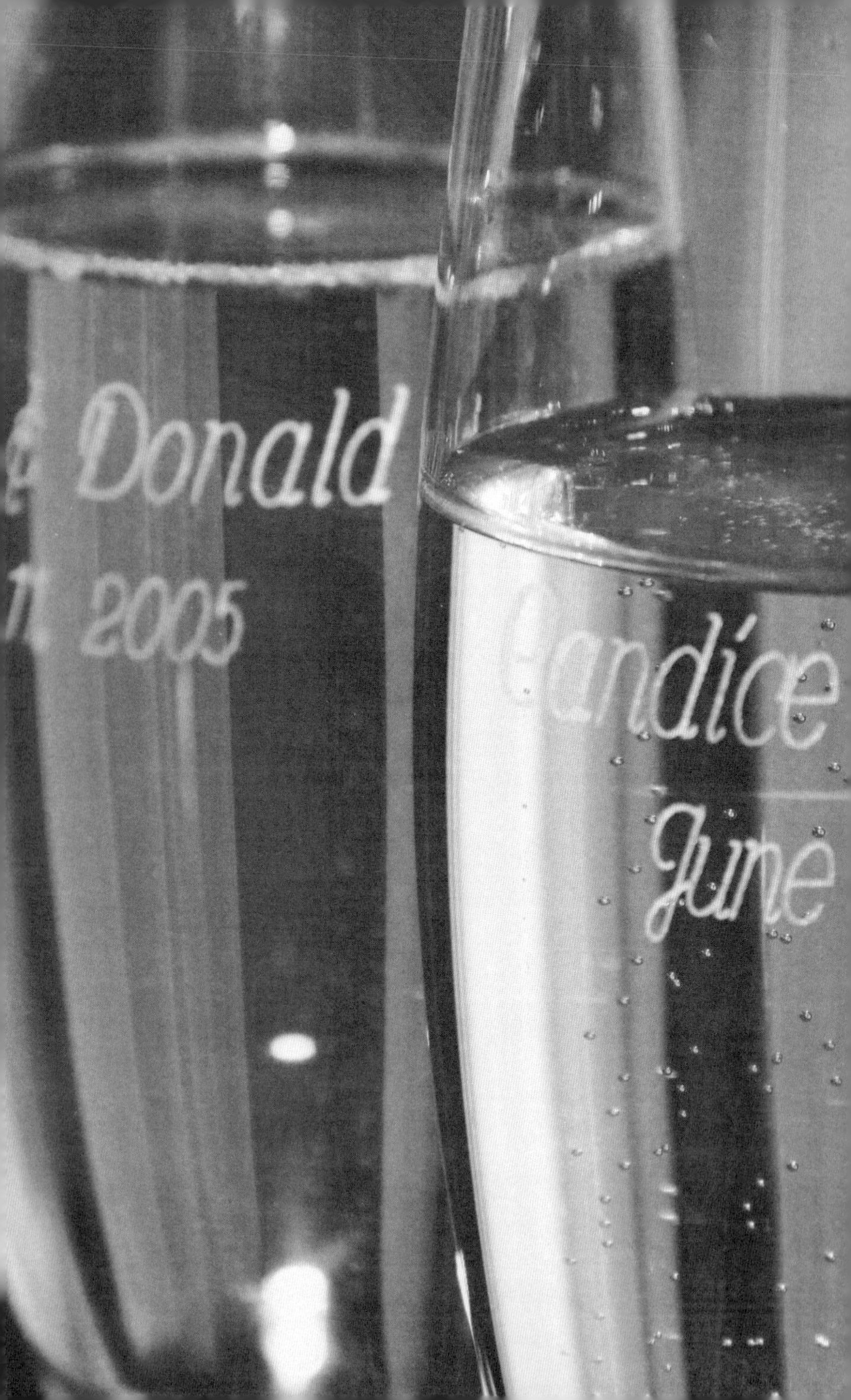
Donald
2005
Candice
June

Eat, drink and be merry

Choosing your caterer

You will find that most venues either have their own caterer or will have a list of preferred suppliers from which you will need to choose your caterer, and so you will not have a huge amount of flexibility. If you do have the scope to choose whomever you want, as with everything else, the best way to find someone good and reliable is to go on personal experience and recommendations. If you decide to go for something outside of normal wedding banquet fare – perhaps to fit in with an oriental or Moroccan theme, for example – ensure that the caterer has experience with this rather than allowing them to use your wedding as an experiment! It will also be worthwhile checking that they have experience of working at your venue, or at least at a similar venue, especially if you are having a marquee wedding. As with all your wedding suppliers, you will want to choose a caterer who is willing to listen to your vision and be flexible both with creativity and cost.

Another big factor when it comes to choosing your caterer is the drink for the drinks reception and meal. Can you supply your own? And if so, how much corkage will they charge? There will normally be a corkage charge per bottle of champagne and another per bottle of wine. This charge may seem a lot to begin with, but when you consider the mark up most caterers will put on a bottle of wine, it may be worth it – you may not actually save yourself any money but you will probably be able to get better quality wine for the same price if you provide it yourself, especially if you buy in bulk from a wine merchants.

Make sure you find out exactly what is included in the price as this can vary from caterer to caterer. You don't want to turn up on the day and realise there are no wine glasses or tablecloths because you were supposed to order them separately! This is particularly important if you are organising a marquee wedding – you will need generators, fridges, cookers and a water supply in addition to the usual tables, chairs, linen, crockery, glassware etc, and you will need to find out as soon as possible who is responsible for providing what. Ask also to see samples of the crockery, cutlery, glassware

Eat, drink and be merry

and linen prior to the event, especially if you are requesting something in a specific colour or style.

Questions to ask... your caterer

- Can we sample the menu/wines beforehand?
- Can we make suggestions for our menu?
- Can you cater for vegans/nut allergies/gluten-free/diabetics?
- Can you provide an evening buffet?
- Will there be a cake cutting fee?
- Can we bring our own wine? What will the corkage charge be?
- Will the wine be placed on the tables or will it be served by the waiting staff?
- What will the ratio of waiting staff to guests be?
- What will the waiting staff be wearing?
- Can you provide coloured tablecloths/chair covers?
- Can you provide matching crockery/glassware in a colour of my choice?
- Can you set up all the name cards/favours/table confetti etc?
- How much time do you need for setting up?
- Do you deal with all the clearing up?
- How much notice do you require for final numbers?
- How much deposit is required and by when?
- When is the final payment due?

Order of the day

The usual order of the day following the ceremony is this: drinks reception, followed by the wedding breakfast, followed by the evening entertainment.

Eat, drink and be merry

Drinks reception

It is usual to have a drinks reception between the ceremony and reception. This allows time for your guests to mix and mingle and keeps them occupied while you are having your photographs taken. If you are opting for more informal, reportage style photographs and aren't planning on spending a long time posing for portraits, then it will give you an extra opportunity to mix and mingle yourself. Your drinks reception shouldn't really last longer than two hours – any longer and your guests may begin to get impatient, hungry and rather worse for wear with drink!

Champagne is still the most popular drink of choice, but there's plenty of scope for being inventive and serving a drink to suit your theme. Mulled wine and eggnog are popular Christmastime choices, a fruity punch would suit a summer wedding, or try lychee martinis for a modern twist. If you have chosen a colour to base your wedding theme around, have fun finding a cocktail that blends in. There are specialist companies who provide fully stocked cocktail bars with professional mixologists if you really want to impress. Talk to your caterer and check how the drinks will be served – will there be waiting staff circling to ensure guests' glasses are kept topped up or will your guests need to go to a central serving area? Whatever you do, make sure there is enough to go round – there is nothing worse than guests hanging around waiting for the next part of the day with no drinks in their hands. People will become restless and it will reflect badly on both your organisational skills and your generosity! If your budget can't stretch to keeping everyone's glasses full for the entire time then organise a pay-bar – better this than no bar at all!

We had a small wedding, only 25 guests, and most of them had flown in from the States for our wedding. So for the drinks reception, we hired a private open-top bus tour round Edinburgh, which everybody loved!

Marcia

Eat, drink and be merry

If you are planning a fairly long drinks reception, particularly if it follows a long ceremony, you may want to provide some kind of food with the drinks. Bear in mind that you will probably be about to serve a proper meal, so nothing too substantial is necessary. Nibbles are a nice touch though and can again be adapted to suit your theme and budget. Strawberries dipped in chocolate make an indulgent accompaniment to champagne or Pimms, mince pies are always appreciated with mulled wine, and mini oriental canapés will finish off that lychee martini very nicely. Whatever you go for, make sure it is easy to serve and easy to eat – nobody wants tomato sauce dribbling down the front of a new wedding outfit! Your caterer will be able to advise on quantities but no more than six canapés per person is normally recommended. How they are served is up to you and your caterer but they are normally served on trays by waiting staff, or alternatively are placed on food stations around the room – depending on the service style of your drinks.

It is a good idea to have some form of background music during the drinks reception – music helps the conversation flow, and will add to the celebratory atmosphere. Jazz bands are popular at this point in the proceedings, as they tend to provide upbeat tunes whilst not being too intruding – they also provide a classy edge to the day. As with everything else though, it's your day, and you should choose music that that will fit in with your theme and personal preferences. If your venue has a suitable sound system you may be able to provide a CD of your favourite tunes, which will obviously be much more cost effective. Or perhaps your piper has a good line in pop songs and could entertain the crowd! As weddings are becoming more varied and the emphasis is shifting towards entertaining your guests, all manner of entertainment is being booked. It is not unusual now to have caricaturists, magicians, or lookalikes mingling with the guests, and it will ensure nobody gets bored while you have your photographs taken.

Eat, drink and be merry

Receiving line

The traditional receiving line has all the bridal party – bride, groom, bridesmaids, best man and both sets of parents lined up to greet the guests as they enter the reception venue. This gives everyone the opportunity to thank the guests for coming, to introduce people and for the guests to thank the hosts for having them. More and more couples are deciding against this, believing it to be more pomp and ceremony than it is worth. It can be awkward too, particularly for the best man and bridesmaids, to have to shake hands and make small talk with a hundred people they don't know. It can also take a long time, leaving your guests either standing in a line for twenty minutes waiting to exchange a few words with you, or sitting at their table waiting for the meal to begin.

If you decide not to have a receiving line, you will need to ensure that you make the effort to go round and speak to every one of your guests at some other point during the day to the thank them for coming, and you will also need to ensure you are introduced to any of your fiancé's family members who you have not yet met. A good compromise is to have a receiving line involving just the two of you. This way you can rest assured that you have spoken to and met everybody, whilst not subjecting the rest of the bridal party to the awkwardness of polite conversation, and you can keep the line moving as quickly as you see fit.

You will need to decide whether to have the receiving line on leaving the drinks reception, or on entering the meal… this will depend on the layout of your venue and the schedule of your day. If you have the receiving line on leaving the drinks reception, it will mean that guests can continue to mingle and have a drink as they wait, rather than standing in line for 20 minutes. On the other hand, having one as they enter the room for the meal will mean you are there to welcome them – you will need to decide what you feel will work best for your wedding.

Eat, drink and be merry

Thanking the piper

It is nice to make an entrance into the reception venue, as this is often the first time you will walk into a room as a married couple. Traditionally you will be announced and then the piper will pipe you to the top table, while everyone stands and claps along. It is customary then for the bride to present the piper with a wee dram of whisky as a token of thanks for his work during the day, as this is normally the last time he will be needed.

Wedding breakfast

So called because it is the first meal you have together as husband and wife, and nothing to do with the time of day it is served, the wedding breakfast can take many forms. How you serve your meal and what you serve will depend on many factors. Your catering company should be able to set their menu options to suit your budget and be helpful with ideas to suit your wedding. Make sure you ask your guests to let you know if they have any specific dietary requirements when replying to your invitation. You should expect at least a handful of vegetarians and have a suitable option. Your catering company will be able to make suggestions.

Top Tip

Work out how much you can afford to spend per head and ask the caterer to show you some sample menus with this figure in mind. You can then start to adapt it to your likes and dislikes.

Factors to consider when planning your wedding breakfast:

Time of day – normally with an early afternoon wedding, by the time the photographs and drinks reception are over, it is late afternoon when you sit down to eat. Obviously not all weddings follow this pattern, and the time of day you have your wedding will impact on what you serve. If you are early risers and go for a

Eat, drink and be merry

morning wedding you could opt for a breakfast in the true sense of the word – how about smoked salmon and scrambled egg served with Bucks Fizz and Bloody Marys? For a summer luncheon you could serve a picnic or buffet on the lawn or how about afternoon tea – a proper high tea with sandwiches, cold meats, trifles, cakes, scones etc.

Time of year – try to adapt your meal to the time of year in which you marry. Warming soups and puddings will be appreciated on a cold winter's day, whilst light soufflés and pavlovas will be more appropriate for a summer celebration. For more unusual approaches, a barbeque or picnic will be more suited to the summer months, while a fondue would be more suitable in the colder months. Remember that using in-season produce will also help keep your costs down.

Type of meal – there are three normal alternatives for serving a wedding breakfast – buffet, semi-buffet or sit-down meal.

For a *buffet*, guests take it in turns to go up to the buffet and help themselves to all the courses. It is a less formal way of serving the meal for a more relaxed reception. It means that your guests can help themselves to exactly what they want and leave what they don't like without having to leave it on their plate! This is normally a cheaper way of serving the meal as less waiting staff are required. Although it gives guests the chance to mingle, it can be disruptive, as guests are continually getting up from their tables, and can take a lot longer as everybody dithers over whether they want the salmon or the beef – and the last table will always feel a little dejected and concerned that there will be nothing left by the time they get there! An alternative is to have food stations around the room, perhaps each with a different theme or course, again encouraging mingling but meaning more people can serve themselves at once.

With a *semi-buffet*, a cold starter will already be on the table when they sit down. The main course is then served as a buffet, with the dessert and coffee served by the waiting staff. This obviously shares

Eat, drink and be merry

many of the pros and cons of the buffet, whilst giving a little more structure to the meal, and will speed things up a bit.

All courses of a *sit-down* meal are served to the guests by the waiting staff. This is the most formal of the three options, will require many more waiting staff but should mean that everybody eats at the same time which will help the meal run much more smoothly.

Top Tip

Be creative with your menu and offer something that your guests won't have had at every other wedding they have been to this year. However, being too adventurous could backfire – you will want to serve something that the majority of people will actually enjoy eating!

Your menu

Your menu is ultimately up to you and your caterer to decide on and will largely depend on the above factors, together with your budget. Do try to offer your guests something a little more imaginative than what is known in the industry as 'conference chicken'. If yours is the fifth wedding of the season for many of your guests, they will enjoy having something different to eat. If you have a favourite meal that isn't traditionally 'wedding' fare, who cares? Kate Winslet famously served sausage and mash at her wedding, so why shouldn't you? Do remember though that your guests have to eat it too and bear in mind that they might not all have the same tastes as you. I have attended one wedding where the steak and kidney pudding had all the guests suddenly announcing they were vegetarian! If you are worried that you may have a particularly fussy set of guests, perhaps you could send the menu out in advance for guests to choose their meal.

Tying in the meal with your theme should help to make your menu unique. Below are some themed menu examples.

Eat, drink and be merry

A Scottish themed wedding

Starter

*Baked filo pastry parcels of haggis (or vegetarian haggis)
served with a Drambuie sauce*

Main Course

*Rump of Aberdeen Angus beef served on clapshot with
a thyme and red wine jus*

or

*Portobello mushroom topped with pesto and
Strathdon Blue cheese*

Dessert

Traditional cranachan served with shortbread and a Glayva syrup

Coffee and tablet

* * *

A Christmas themed wedding

Starter

Carrot and nutmeg soup

Main Course

Turkey and chestnut roulade with a boozy cranberry sauce

or

Chestnut and cranberry loaf with a boozy cranberry sauce

Dessert

Christmas pudding ice cream served in a brandy snap basket

Coffee and mints

Eat, drink and be merry

A medieval banquet wedding

Starter

French onion soup served with gruyere-topped french bread

Main Course

Suckling pig, roast chicken and lamb cutlets served with baked potatoes, roast corn and vegetables

or

Vegetable kebabs with a peppercorn sauce served with baked potatoes and roast corn

Dessert

Individual meringues topped with whipped cream and fruits of the forest

Coffee and wedding cake

* * *

Oriental themed wedding

Starter

Vegetable spring rolls with hoisin dipping sauce

Main Course

Glazed duck served with a mange tout, baby corn and beansprout salad

or

Quorn noodle nests served with a Chinese greens and cashew stirfry

Dessert

Passionfruit and mango mousse

Coffee and fortune cookies

Top tips for choosing your wine

- Taste the wine yourself, don't rely on other people's opinions – why not organise a wine tasting with a few friends for a fun night out? Many wine merchants will do this for you, and a good wine merchant will be able to advise on what will match your menu.

- Have a trial run – if you're not sure about your choice, order a case and try it out on some friends.

- Be sure to try the wine out with the meal you will be serving to check they complement one another.

- See if you can negotiate a discount for a bulk order.

- Avoid brand names unless you are a committed fan – everyone will know how much it costs and someone will be sure to comment!

- Avoid particularly strong flavoured wines – many people dislike heavily oaked chardonnays, sweet whites and overly robust reds.

- Many wine merchants will sell you wine on a sale or return basis, meaning you can order more than enough safe in the knowledge that you can return any unopened bottles.

Seating plan

So your Auntie Mary and Uncle Bill aren't on speaking terms, your brother won't tolerate Manchester United fans, and your fiancé's best mate is likely to tell crude jokes once he's had a few too many glasses of wine… organising the seating plan is the part that everyone dreads and which causes more headaches than any other aspects of the planning!

Top table

Traditionally the top table is a long table set at the top of the room facing the other tables, with the traditional seating order as follows:

Eat, drink and be merry

(from the left) chief bridesmaid, father of the groom, mother of the bride, groom, bride, father of the bride, mother of the groom, best man. Many people decide against a long top table – it is not a particularly sociable way of eating, and people feel awkward feeling like they are 'on show'. If you are having speeches after the meal, making the best man sit through his meal feeling like all eyes are on him will only add to his nerves and will not allow him to relax and enjoy his meal. A round top table is therefore becoming more popular – it will mean a more sociable and relaxed meal for you and you can position yourself in amongst your guests to feel more a part of it. You can still set it apart from the others by giving it a different look – perhaps a different coloured tablecloth or a more dramatic table centre, or even having it on a raised platform.

If you have difficult family politics, you could opt for a small top table for just the two of you – it will give you the opportunity to sit and enjoy each other's company for a while on the day without feeling obliged to rush around talking to all the guests. Another option, for a smaller wedding, is to have all the guests' tables at right angles to the top table, forming a large square so you really are in amongst it.

Guests

The most difficult step is trying to seat all your guests at tables, if indeed you are having a fixed table plan. Remember that they will be sitting here for a good couple of hours, and you want them to enjoy themselves as much as possible, so the more thought you put into your seating plan the better. This is a good opportunity to encourage your guests to mingle and get to know one another. People will naturally spend most of the day catching up with others they know, so for the couple of hours during the meal it is nice to bring your different groups of friends together – half the fun of weddings is getting to know new people, after all. Obviously it is advisable to try to match like-minded people, and you will always be thanked for sitting single friends together – there's nothing like a good bit of flirting at a wedding! It is generally advisable not to mix the age groups together too much, although you should know all your guests well enough to judge who will get along with whom.

An easy (well, it'll never be easy!) way of working out your table plan is this: write out the names of all your guests onto separate pieces of paper, or into an Excel spreadsheet and divide them up into groups (ie. your school friends, his school friends, your college friends, his college friends etc.) You can then sit down together and start sorting people from each group into tables of eight or ten or however many people you have decided on per table. It will take time and several attempts but at least if you have organised it this way, it is easy to shift people from one table to another without having to keep rewriting lists.

Numbered or named?

The standard practice is to number your tables, so that it is quick and easy for your guests to identify where they will be sitting. It is becoming more common now to name your tables instead, as this does away with the 'hierarchy' problem. You can choose names either to tie in with your theme (perhaps Scottish islands for a Scottish theme) or with something that is personal to you (favourite songs or films).

It is helpful to have a table plan (or two, depending on your numbers) either at the entrance to the room where the meal is to be served, and/or in the drinks reception area. Check if your venue can provide this, or you could make it yourself to tie in with your stationery or theme.

Speeches

Traditionally, speeches are given after the meal, once coffee has been served, although it is becoming more common now for the speeches to precede the meal. It is entirely up to you and both options have their obvious pros and cons.

If, for example, your best man is particularly nervous about giving his speech, it can make for a very long and not particularly

Eat, drink and be merry

enjoyable meal if all he can think about is the fact that he has to get up and perform at the end of it. Either this or he will over-indulge on the wine to calm his nerves – clearly neither situation is particularly desirable! Having the speeches before the meal can therefore allow everybody to relax and enjoy the rest of the evening.

However, your guests will normally be more receptive to the speeches *after* the meal – they will be well fed, (meaning they won't be wondering how much longer until they can eat!) and well watered (meaning they will be more likely to laugh along with the jokes!). There is always a real feeling of anticipation during the meal about the speeches and it is a good way to signal the end of the formal part of the day and the beginning of the party. Having the speeches at the end of the meal tends to be favoured by catering companies also, as they are not waiting around keeping the food warm while the speeches drag on and on.

There are plenty of books specialising in the subject of wedding speeches and it is also worth checking out www.hitched.co.uk for example speeches. However, the order and contents are briefly described below:

Order of speeches and toasts

Father of the bride – welcomes the groom to the family, says a few words about his daughter (normally how proud of her he and his wife are, embellished with a few funny anecdotes from her life) and ends with a toast to the bride and groom.

Groom – thanks his new father-in-law for his kind words, says thank yous to all who have been involved, gives out thank you presents/bouquets to the mothers and/or helpers, says a few words about his new wife, and ends with a toast to the bridesmaids.

Best man – thanks the groom for his kind words on behalf of the bridesmaids, reads messages, tells anecdotes about the groom, and normally ends with a final toast either to absent friends or to the bride and groom.

Eat, drink and be merry

Additional speeches

Bride – nearly half of all brides now like to add their own speech to the order of proceedings. Obviously it is entirely up to you if you feel comfortable doing this or whether you would prefer to just sit back and let your new husband speak on behalf of you both.

The beauty of a bride's speech is that it is still a relatively new addition to wedding tradition and therefore you are less bound by etiquette... meaning anything goes! You can choose where your speech would fit in best – though the most common is after the father of the bride's speech. You can also choose what you want to say and who you wish to toast, with common bridal toasts being 'to absent friends', or 'to the guests!'

Bridesmaid – if you're a stickler for equality you may wish to allow your bridesmaid to thank the best man herself for his kind words. She will also be in a better position to recount stories about you in recent years.

Master of ceremonies – it may be a nice touch to have a close friend or relative perform the role of master of ceremonies. This will allow him or her to add their own personal touch to the proceedings, perhaps adding their own anecdotes to the introductions and in-between slots.

One thing to remember though is that the more people you have speaking, the more important it is to keep them short. None of your guests will enjoy sitting through five half-hour speeches, no matter how moving or funny they are. Also worth bearing in mind is that the more people you have speaking, the greater the chance of stories being repeated – you will all need to check that you don't overlap.

Entertainment

Music during the meal

Having some background music can help aid conversation during the meal, and helps avoid any awkward silences. However, you will need to choose something fairly unobtrusive, whether this be a live

Eat, drink and be merry

string quartet or a CD, you don't want people to be shouting over the music to be heard.

After-dinner entertainment

The most popular choices for after-dinner entertainment are a live band or a DJ. When choosing your entertainment, bear in mind that you will probably have a wide range of tastes to accommodate, from your college friends to your great aunt and uncle and you want everyone to enjoy themselves. There are many bands that specialise in wedding entertainment, doing cover songs from the last fifty years so that there is something for everyone. A good wedding entertainer will be able to judge what is going down particularly well and adapt their repertoire to suit.

Ceilidh bands are still a popular choice for Scottish weddings – they are a great way to get everyone on the dance floor and encourage mingling amongst guests. If you are going to have lots of guests from outwith Scotland, it is a good idea to have a caller to ensure everyone knows what they are doing. Several wedding bands will be able to play a few of the more popular ceilidh dances in addition to more contemporary tunes, and this is becoming a popular compromise.

As with everything else in the wedding world, a good way of choosing a band is on personal experience and recommendations. It can also be a good idea, for your own peace of mind, to book a band or DJ through an agency – this way if anything should happen to the band or DJ you have booked, they will be able to substitute them for another. If you are really worried, it may be a good idea to take along a selection of party CDs, or an iPod with a playlist, and ensure there is a sound system in the room, just to be safe.

First dance

Traditionally nobody dances until the bride and groom have hit the dance floor to open the evening's festivities. You may decide to go for something traditional like a Gay Gordon's to get the ceilidh started or you may choose to go for something more personal.

Eat, drink and be merry

Perhaps you have 'a song', which you would like to be your first dance together as a married couple, or you have a favourite track, which you think would be particularly appropriate. If you have the time and energy you could start taking dance classes now and really wow your guests with a surprise tango or cha cha cha!

If neither of you are particularly comfortable with the idea of dancing alone in front of everyone, you do have other options – perhaps you could start off the dance for a few moments and then invite the rest of your wedding party to join you (if you brief the band on this beforehand they will be able to help you out by calling people to the dance floor). Traditionally the bride's mother dances the first dance with the groom's father and vice versa, the best man dances with the chief bridesmaid and you can match up any remaining groomsmen and bridesmaids. Or alternatively you could start the fun off with a conga around the room and get everyone to join in. You shouldn't really skip the first dance unless you make it very clear to everyone that you are going to – you don't want everyone sitting around an empty dance floor all night because they didn't want to be first up there before the happy couple!

Something a bit different

Entertainment is becoming more diverse at weddings so dare to be daring and give your guests something to talk about in the weeks to follow. You can hire lookalikes to mingle with your guests over champagne, magicians who will entertain with up-close tricks and caricaturists who will capture your unsuspecting guests over dinner. For raucous after-dinner fun, how about organising a bucking bronco, oversize sumo wrestling or a jousting tournament? For something a bit tamer, you could set up casino tables around the room and offer a prize for the most successful gambler.

Don't forget the children

If you know there are going to be lots of children at the wedding, it may be worth employing a children's entertainer for the evening – they will appreciate being catered for and it will keep them out of

Eat, drink and be merry

their parents' hair, allowing them have a great time too. A bouncy castle will keep them (and probably a few adults) entertained for hours!

Mingling with your guests

You will want to try and ensure you spend some time with everyone, but don't get too bogged down with this – you need to relax and have a good time as well. People will understand that you don't have huge amounts of time to spend with them – if you have a hundred guests and only spend two minutes with each, it will take you over three hours! Don't be surprised if you are the one making all the effort to go and talk to people either. Even your closest friends will tend to keep their distance and wait for you to come to them, thinking you're too busy to be bothered.

'I woke up the next day, and while I had had a fantastic time at the wedding, I couldn't really remember having been alone with Alec once the whole day, or even really spending much time with him at all!'

Shona

Don't forget either, why you're there in the first place… make sure you spend some time with your new husband!

Make sure you spend some quality time together. Take a moment to stop and look around together, enjoy each other's company over the meal, take a few minutes on your own after the photos, go and mingle with your guests together, and if all else fails, drag him off to the dance floor every now and then!

Hey, good looking!

Every bride wants to look her absolute best on her wedding day – after all everyone will be looking at you, and will continue to look at the photos for years to come. However, there is more to looking your best than a fabulous dress and a good makeup artist – and you may want to start the beauty preparations now!

Hey, good looking!

Lifestyle

Your ideal pre-wedding lifestyle could be summed up in three simple words – relaxation, sleep and exercise.

Relaxation – It is essential that you allow time in your diary for relaxation in the lead up to the big day – your stress levels will probably be higher than normal, which, if you're not careful, will leave you with bad skin and lacklustre hair. As you plan your wedding, it will begin to take over your life, but try to plan time when you and your fiancé can go and do something non-wedding related that will really take your mind off things. A day at a health spa, a walk and some fresh air, or even an evening at the cinema will do wonders for your soul.

Sleep – The time that you are asleep is when your body does all its healing, so if you don't get enough of it, it will begin to show in your skin and hair, not to mention those bags under your eyes… it's not called 'beauty sleep' for nothing! Aim for early nights in the lead up to your wedding.

Exercise – Exercising will give your circulation a major boost, helping to flush away the toxins that cause blemishes. Once you get into a routine, not only will you begin to look more toned and healthy but you will notice a general upturn in your feeling of well-being and the amount of energy you have. It will do wonders for your stress levels too. If you don't already have a routine exercise regimen, aim to get started about six months before the big day. Start gently and work your way up. If you join a gym, a personal trainer will often be on hand to set up a programme for you, giving you achievable goals to get the results you want. If you don't think you have the self-motivation to stick to a programme, find a gym that offers classes, as this way you'll be encouraged to keep going when you would normally give up. If the thought of a gym makes you shudder – try something else. Swimming is great exercise, or try dancing, tennis or squash. If even this sounds like your worst nightmare, then try ditching the bus or car in the morning and walking to work. Half an hour of brisk walking a day and you'll begin to notice the results in just a few weeks.

Hey, good looking!

Diet

Only you will know what your ideal weight is and how you want to look on your wedding day. If you do plan to lose weight before your wedding, try to do it sensibly and remember that if you do lose weight quickly and in the last few weeks before the day, you may end up having to have your dress adjusted. The most sensible advice is to eat a healthy and balanced diet – plenty of fresh fruit and vegetables (remember five portions a day is recommended) will give you all those essential vitamins that are good for your skin, hair, nails and general well-being. A great way to start the day is with a bowl of fresh fruit salad or try a homemade breakfast smoothie (see below). Try to avoid excessive alcohol intake in the few weeks before the wedding (difficult with a hen night on the horizon, I know!), and try and cut down on that smoking habit! Replace chocolates and crisps with fresh fruit when you fancy a snack, and drink lots of water – eight glasses a day is the recommended amount, to flush away the toxins.

Breakfast smoothie – serves two

1 banana
6 large strawberries
3 tablespoons of yoghurt
1 small glass of orange juice
1 small glass of pineapple juice

Simply put all the ingredients in a blender and blend until smooth.

Skin

If you don't have a proper skincare regime, you should aim to start at least six months before the wedding. All experts seem to agree that a routine of cleanse, tone and moisturise is the way to go, with weekly exfoliation and facemasks thrown in for good measure. If your budget allows, consider booking yourself in for a monthly facial in the lead up the big day too… not only will it benefit your skin, but it is wonderfully relaxing and will help keep your stress levels under control as well. If you do plan to try facials for the first

Hey, good looking!

time, ensure you do so a few months before the wedding – having one a few days before could result in a blotchy face. Plan to have your last one about a week before the wedding day.

Hair

If you want your hair a certain way for your wedding, you will need to start planning ahead to ensure it is the right length and/or right cut for the look you are going for. You will know yourself what your hair is like, but most hair takes about two weeks from being cut to settle, and so if it is a certain cut you are going for, aim to have the final haircut approximately two weeks before your wedding day – you can always pop back for a touch up the morning of, or day before, the wedding if needs be.

If you are trying something new, and/or going for an elaborate up-do, book in for a trial with the hairdresser a couple of months before to ensure you are going to like the look you are going for. Make sure you have your tiara and/or hair accessories in time for this trial. Most brides like to grow their hair in anticipation of the big day, and opt for an up-do. If you are having your hair put up for the day, most hairdressers will tell you not to wash your hair on the morning of the wedding as it will not be as easy to work with. If you can't be bothered to grow your hair but still fancy the thought of a fancy up-do, consider having hair extensions fitted – if it's good enough for Victoria Beckham, it's good enough for you! You needn't have expensive extensions fitted either, as your hairdresser could attach a hair-piece just for the day if necessary. Talk it through with your hairdresser and have fun experimenting with your new look!

Top Tip

Wear a front-fastening top when having your hair and makeup done on the morning of your wedding, so you don't ruin your look when getting undressed.

Hey, good looking!

Be sure to keep your hair in good condition in the lead up to the wedding day – regular haircuts (every six to eight weeks) are important to avoid split ends, even if you are trying to grow your hair, and remember that excessive use of hairdryers and straighteners will also damage your hair. If you do have dry or damaged hair, you may want to treat yourself with a nourishing mask every week in the last few weeks before the wedding.

Nails

It is essential to have good nails on your wedding day – everyone will be admiring your ring and there will be close up photos of your hands as you sign the marriage schedule, cut the cake, hold hands with your new husband etc. Try to keep your nails in good condition in the months leading up to your wedding, and go for (or give yourself) a weekly manicure. If you really can't grow your nails to a length that you are happy with, have some false nails fitted – they can look very realistic. The colour you paint them will depend on your overall look, but most brides normally opt for a French manicure for their wedding day. And don't forget your toes – especially if you are wearing open shoes – a pedicure before your wedding will ensure you have nice looking feet for your honeymoon too!

Make-up

When it comes to make-up, most brides prefer a natural look for their wedding day. Once again however, it is down to personal taste and preference. If you normally wear heavy make-up, you may not feel comfortable going for a more natural look. Most make-up artists advise applying your make-up as you would for a black-tie event, making more effort than you would for a day in the office, but nothing too trendy or over-the-top.

If you are not comfortable doing your own make-up for your wedding day, you will need to find a make-up artist. Many makeup artists specialise in wedding make-up and will travel to you on the morning of the wedding. It is a good idea to arrange a trial with the

Hey, good looking!

make-up artist for a few weeks before the wedding to ensure you are happy with the style. Alternatively, try make-up counters in your local department stores – Bobbi Brown counters offer make-up lessons, and all their counter staff are either trained, or are in training as make-up artists. Space NK also train all their staff as make-up artists, and they will do you a trial, and note which products are used so you can recreate the look on the day. They do charge for this, but the charge is redeemable against any purchases. It is worth asking around the department stores, as you may find someone who will agree to do a trial, and then repeat the look on the morning of the wedding.

However you decide to have your make-up applied, make sure you buy some of the products used, in particular the lipstick and powder, for touch-ups during the day.

It's a wrap!

Whether you opt for fine china, a cellar full of wine, or contributions towards your honeymoon, one of the most indulgent things about the big day preparations is putting together the wedding list… and the choice of gifts has never been better.

Gift list etiquette

Many couples feel awkward about the prospect of putting together a wedding list, fearing they will appear rude and greedy. To the contrary, the majority of your guests will be thankful to have some guidance and be happy in the knowledge that they are buying you something that you actually want. A wedding list is very much the norm these days and is seen as a practical way of ensuring you receive what you want – and more importantly, not four or five of what you don't want! It is perfectly acceptable, and indeed expected, nowadays to include information relating to your list (normally in the form of a notification card supplied by your gift list provider) with your invitations.

Do think of your guests as well as yourselves when putting together your list, and be sure to include a variety of gifts. It is sensible to choose a range of items, to include things you really need, in addition to other more unusual or frivolous gifts – perhaps that cocktail bar set you don't actually need but would look great on your sideboard! Older relatives may like buying you the more practical items such as linen or cutlery but your younger, funkier friends will prefer to buy you something a bit more creative. Make sure you cater for all budgets too, so that no matter how much or how little your guests want to spend, they can find something to buy you. It is usually a good idea to put some additional vouchers on the list too. Don't worry about putting very expensive items on your list – you may find that some people will club together to buy something larger. It is also a good idea to put multiple small gifts on there too as it means people can mix and match if they want.

Present showing

It is customary in Scotland to have a present showing where all the gifts are unwrapped and displayed. All the women who have given gifts are invited round to an 'open house' day where refreshments are served and the bride shows the guests around to see her gifts. It is a less common custom nowadays, but some mothers may still insist on it.

It's a wrap!

The choice is yours

The face of modern wedding lists is changing. With more and more couples living together prior to marriage, and people tending to marry later in life, many couples are finding that they have all the household items they need and are looking for other, less traditional gift list options. Although department stores such as John Lewis remain the most popular provider of wedding lists in Britain, several other companies are gaining in popularity, offering an even wider choice of gifts. At Wrapit, for example, you can include all the toasters and dinner plates you want, in addition to a golfing weekend, a row of vines in a French vineyard and a helicopter trip in London. Alternatively if you are keen gardeners, you could have your list at the Wedding Garden Company where you can include plants and garden-related products.

If you want to steer away from household items altogether, how about a honeymoon wedding list? With an estimated four in ten couples now asking for money towards their honeymoon in place of traditional gifts, a honeymoon wedding list makes perfect sense. Companies such as HoneyMoney provide a wedding list which divides up your honeymoon itinerary into affordable portions so that your friends and family can buy you anything from a night in a hotel or a romantic meal, to an elephant safari or hot air balloon ride. This means that not only do you avoid the awkward situation of asking people for money, but your guests feel that they are actually buying you a tangible gift – and hopefully one that you will remember forever! This especially makes sense for couples who are paying for their own wedding and find that there is little or no money left over for the honeymoon. Many travel agents will also allow your guests to buy travel vouchers towards your honeymoon.

Another idea for the couple who really has everything is to have a charity gift list. There are a few companies who do this, where you can either set your list up for donations to a preferred charity or you can include separate gifts for several charities – donations could be for anything from a first aid kit to an eye operation, to a tree being planted. It's a good way to give something back!

The Internet

The internet is another major factor in the changing face of wedding lists. Gone are the days when your guests would travel to the shop, browse the shelves for the ideal gift, stand in the checkout queue, carry it home and wrap it for themselves, then bring it along to hand over to you personally! Nowadays you can often choose your gifts, set up your gift list, your guests can buy from it and your gifts will be delivered, all without any of you having to leave the comfort of your own home! It is well worth at least providing this service as an option to your guests, and if you can do this, it will help take the stress out of your organising the list also, although many department stores still prefer you to go round the store with a scanner.

Things to consider

You will want to find a company that is easy to use – easy for you to set up your list, easy for your guests to buy from the list, easy to check the status of your list, and easy for you to receive your gifts.

Easy for you to set up – Can you go round the shop with a scanner to create your list? Can you set up your list online? Will the company provide notification cards for you to include with your invitations?

Easy for your guests – Does the shop have nationwide branches or is it specific to your town? Can your guests browse your list and buy online? Will the company organise wrapping, packing and postage? Can your guests buy over the phone? Will your list be easy to find? Remember that not all your guests will know both your surnames and have your personal reference number with them at all times – the easier your list is to find, the more presents you are likely to receive!

Easy to check the status – how will you know who has bought you what? Can you go online and check the status? Will you receive an email every time someone buys you a gift? This can be very important if you want to write thank you letters as you go, or

It's a wrap!

if you need to see how much money you are accumulating towards your honeymoon, for example.

Easy to receive your gifts – how will your gifts be delivered? As they are bought, or in one delivery following the wedding? What happens if items become out of stock? And what happens with gifts that aren't bought – can you buy them yourselves at a discounted rate? (This is especially important if you are left with only half a dinner service, for example). Will you have an option to exchange the gifts you have been bought for others you perhaps wish you had been bought?

Girls behaving badly!

Everyone deserves a good send-off from single life and, like weddings, hen and stag nights are becoming more and more elaborate affairs. Whereas once a night in the local pub with all your friends would suffice, these days weekends away, even abroad, are becoming the norm.

Girls behaving badly!

Who does what?

Traditionally it is your chief bridesmaid and best man's responsibility to organise the hen and stag night respectively. It is up to you (and depends on how trusting you are!) as to how involved you become in the organisation. The important thing is for you to enjoy yourself – far too many people see the hen and stag nights as an excuse to 'punish' their friends and make a fool of them, making them wear ridiculous clothes and drink ridiculous drinks. This is your last chance to have a great night out with all your friends together as a single girl – make sure they allow you to have the best time possible… and if this means setting down some ground rules, so be it. If you know that dressing up as a French maid will ruin your evening or you cringe at the thought of a scantily clad man smothered in baby oil gyrating in front of you, make sure those organising the night know this.

Even if you do want to become involved in organising your hen night, it is a good idea to hand over the majority of the responsibility to someone else – you will be run off your feet with the rest of your wedding planning and you will probably be relieved to have someone else take over for a while. And, if it still all sounds like too much trouble, there are plenty of companies out there specialising in hen and stag weekends who can organise and book everything for you.

Feet washing

Feet washing is an old Scottish ceremony, rarely practised nowadays. The night before the wedding, friends and family would turn up at the respective houses of the bride and groom to carry out the feet washing. The bride's feet would be washed in a tub into which her mother would drop a ring. All the girls would then search frantically to find the ring, and the winner would be deemed the next to marry. (Similar to the bouquet tossing of today.)

What's your style?

We've all seen the groups of girls wearing devil's horns, traipsing

Girls behaving badly!

in and out of pubs behind a bride-to-be, dressed to the nines in L-plates, flashing tiara, coloured veil, dragging a ball and chain, with a blow up male doll under her arm. This all too common sight characterises the typical hen night in Britain these days. However, for every bride that thinks this sounds like the ideal way to see out her single years, there's another that cringes at the thought, and hen nights involving spa packages, civilised dinners and shopping weekends away are becoming more popular. With the massive boom in hen and stag nights, there is more and more pressure to organise something different and memorable, and you will want this to be a special time for you to remember.

Hen nights with a difference

A Sporting Occasion – check the sporting calendar and see if anything grabs your fancy – perhaps a day at Wimbledon coiffing champagne? Or a flutter at the races? Or a night at the dogs?

Activity Day – karting, paintballing, off-road driving, white-water rafting – who says it's only for the boys?

Murder Mystery Evening – several country hotels offer packages, which include your accommodation, meal and entertainment. Or you can buy it in a box like a board game – just open ahead of time to give everyone their characters and dress up for an evening full of fun!

Slumber Party – several chic hotels are cashing in on the girly hen night phenomenon. Packages include your accommodation, food, chick flick movie hire, champagne and in-room pampering.

Casino Evening – why not get dressed up and try your luck on the black jack or roulette tables?

Local Festivals – entertainment on a plate. How about running with the bulls in Pamplona? Or the Munich Beer Festival? Or maybe getting muddy at Glastonbury?

The Blackening

The blackening is a ceremony that is still traditionally carried out to the groom (although nowadays it may happen to an unlucky bride) in parts of Scotland, particularly in the Highland and rural regions.

Girls behaving badly!

The groom is captured by his friends, bound and then 'blackened' using a messy mixture, usually containing treacle, flour and feathers. He is then either left somewhere far from home to find his way back, or is paraded around town on the back of a lorry for all to see, accompanied by much noise. The origin of this tradition is believed to be linked to the feet washing ceremony (see above), as when this was being carried out, the groom's feet and legs were often smeared with grease, soot etc.

Get away!

Cheap, no-frills airlines mean that a weekend away in Europe can now work out as cheap as staying in Britain if you choose a city that is inexpensive once you get there. What you spend on the flight can often be counteracted in the price of accommodation and entertainment. Destinations such as Prague, Tallinn and other Eastern European cities are renowned for being cheap, but on the other hand, if your budget is tight, you'd be advised to avoid Scandinavia.

You will need to consider your priorities – is going somewhere far-flung and unusual the most important thing to you? Or does the location not matter, as long as all your friends can make it? Las Vegas for a week may sound like a great idea, but if you go along this route, expect that several of your friends will not be able to afford to join you. On the other hand, if you would prefer to keep it intimate, this could be a way of controlling your numbers. It's lovely to have as many friends with you as possible, but if you are planning a weekend away, organising flights, accommodation, entertainment etc. for a very large group will prove to be a logistical nightmare – just trying to organise dinner for the group could tip you over the edge! If you are planning something on the more expensive side, it's a good idea to give your friends as much notice as possible, so that they can start saving for it. Also, if it includes a weekday, most will appreciate being given lots of warning to plan taking any time off work.

Before you put your itinerary together you should consider who will be coming – will it just be your young and trendy girlfriends?

Girls behaving badly!

Or are your Mum, Gran and Great Auntie Mabel likely to be joining in the fun too? This will obviously have an impact on the activities you are planning.

Tips for the organiser

The planning procedure

Unless you are used to organising groups of people and booking travel, accommodation and activities, planning a hen night could cause you a headache. Below are some tips on making the planning procedure as pain-free as possible.

Before the event:

- Email everyone as early as possible with idea of itinerary and cost – give them a RSVP date and ask for them to let you know whether they are coming or not so that you have an idea of numbers before you continue.

- Get the money in – either ask them to send a deposit with their response, or let them know how much money will be due and when. Don't book anything until you have had at least a deposit from people – if they change their minds and decide not to go, you'll end up having to pay out of your own pocket. It may be worth opening a separate credit card, preferably one with 0% interest for a fixed term, which will last you until the hen night. That way you can pay for things easily and then use other people's money to pay off the credit card without you actually incurring any interest.

- Research – research your destination *thoroughly*. A good tour is one that has been well thought out. The Internet is your best friend when it comes to researching destinations. You can research flights, accommodation, local activities, bars, restaurants, spas, shops – everything a girl needs for a good time! The Lonely Planet website has a chat forum where you can ask the advice of others who have been there before you, and the tripadvisor website has readers' reviews and links to articles for various hotels and destinations. The 'Itchy' websites are also a good way of researching British cities. Companies who specialise in organising hen night packages are a good source of information – even if you decide against using them, their websites will give you good ideas of what there is to do in your chosen destination.

- Establish the itinerary – be organised, especially if there are a lot of hens in your group – pre-book everything and don't leave any choices to people – just tell them where they are going and when, or nobody will make a decision and you'll end up arguing and dithering and not going anywhere at all.
Organise activities for both day and night – variety will keep everyone entertained. Don't forget meal times or everyone will be on the floor after their first cosmopolitan! Ensure you work in a time for breakfast, lunch and dinner, and if necessary make bookings, especially if you are a large group. Check dress codes for any bars or clubs you intend to go to and see if you can get on the guest list for the place you intend on ending your night. If you can't, find out what time they get busy and make sure you get in well before then.

Once you're there:

- Start a kitty – having a kitty means nobody gets landed with a round of expensive cocktails for 20 people, while someone else skulks in the background drinking for free all night. It also encourages the group to stick together. Just make sure someone responsible is in charge of it!

- Give everyone a copy of the itinerary, and make sure it includes the organiser's mobile phone number and details of your accommodation, in case anyone gets lost.

- Theming – having a theme for the night/weekend is a good way to form immediate bonding in a group. Whether you go for full seventies dressing up or the clichéd devil's horns, it is a good way of breaking the ice and puts everyone in a fun mood – and also means you can easily identify members of your group.
Do be sure to check that it won't stop you getting into any of the pubs, clubs or restaurants you are planning on going to.

Get away!

The common image of a honeymoon destination is white sands, azure waters and two palm trees with a double hammock between them. But it doesn't have to be! Although this is still the majority of newlyweds' idea of the perfect post-wedding getaway, more and more couples are shunning the typical beach resort honeymoon for other more varied options. With world-wide travel now easier and more affordable than ever before, the world really is your oyster!

Photograph: Barry Duncan

Beach bliss

If the above picture postcard scene is your ideal, you will be spoilt for choice of tour operators waiting to help realise your dream. Many of the top companies advertise in bridal magazines, or you can find their brochures at your local travel agents, or by doing a search on the web. There are several companies who specialise in luxury holidays and honeymoons and your honeymoon may be your one chance to splash out and enjoy the exclusive far-flung resorts that these companies can offer.

Before you book, ensure you know exactly what is included in the cost, and what will be charged as extra, and if possible see if you can get hold of a copy of the rates of any additional items (activities, spa treatments, drinks etc.). Does all-inclusive really mean all-inclusive, or will there be an additional charge for certain drinks, meal upgrades or activities? Watch too for resorts offering fantastic low-cost half board rates (where breakfast and dinner is included). You may find that their lunch and drink prices are exorbitant, and if you have no alternative for two weeks you will soon watch your budget spiral out of control.

Think carefully about what kind of holiday you really want. Are you happy to lie on the beach for a whole two weeks, or would you actually prefer the option of exploring the surrounding area, or a few days scuba diving? This will obviously affect the resort you choose. Be sure to read up on the range of facilities carefully too – will you really be happy eating in the same restaurant and drinking in the same bar ten nights in a row? And if you want *total* peace and relaxation, check what the policy on children is.

Multi-destination holidays

If you fear stopping in one resort for the entire holiday will give you cabin fever, perhaps a multi-destination holiday will be more to you liking. Several companies provide multi-stop packages, allowing you a change of scenery. Thailand is a popular destination for this kind of holiday, where you can combine a trip to bustling Bangkok, with

Get away!

elephant trekking in Chiang Mai, and then kick back on the sands of Koh Samui. Holidays in Africa and the Indian Ocean are perfect for combining the adventure of safari with the relaxation of the beach, or how about Central America for a reef and rainforest multi-stop honeymoon?

Several companies will be happy to tailor-make a package for you based on your preferences, allowing you complete control over your itinerary, but without the hassle of having to individually book flights, hotels, transfers etc.

Cruises are making a big comeback and provide a relaxing and enjoyable way to visit several places. There are hundreds of cruise companies operating so you should be able to find something to suit you. The Cruise Information Service website is a good place to start, providing information on which companies cruise where, together with contact details and links. And before you book, you may want to read a few personal customer reviews. The Cruise Opinion website holds over 5,000!

Top Tip

Don't forget you will need spending money! Don't spend your entire budget on the package and then find that you can't afford to buy or do anything once you are there. Make sure you allow a generous budget for spending money so you can indulge in a little luxury while you are there – after all, it is your honeymoon!

Activity and adventure

If you yawn at the thought of a relaxing beach holiday, you could join hundreds of other newlyweds who opt for an adventure to remember for their honeymoon. Trekking the Inca Trail to Machu Picchu, whitewater rafting the Zambezi, hanging with the orang-utans in Borneo or sea kayaking in Vietnam are just a few of the once-in-a-lifetime experiences on offer. Several companies specialise in these types of holidays, allowing you to see more of a country than just its coastline and ensuring you have a great laugh

at the same time, with memories to last with you forever.
Some tours can be group-based, meaning little quality time for
you and your new hubby, but most companies will re-work your
itinerary meaning you can perhaps combine a week trekking with
a group, with a week in an exclusive jungle lodge for just the
two of you. If you have a particular activity in mind try
www.adventuredirectory.com and www.wild-dog.com, both of
which allow you to search by activity and region and then link to
tour operators providing these tours.

Even if you are an adventure-mad couple and hate the thought of a
'relaxing' holiday, it is worth bearing in mind that you are likely to
be exhausted after the excitement of the wedding, so at least a few
days of total relaxation will probably be a welcome break.

Go it alone

The growth of the Internet means that it is easier now than it ever
has been to put together your own itinerary and organise your own
dream honeymoon, giving you maximum flexibility to do what you
want to do, where you want to do it.

Reading travel brochures is often a good place to start, to get an
idea of highlights of the different destinations and realistic
itineraries. Once you have chosen your dream destination, go out
and buy a couple of guidebooks – e.g. Lonely Planet, Rough Guide
or Fodor's guide – and do your research by visiting the country's
tourist information site. Pick out places you think you would like to
visit and places you would like to stay, and check them out on the
Internet to find out more. Log onto the Lonely Planet's Thorn Tree
forum, or the Bootsnall forum to ask other travellers' advice, or
read reviews on tripadvisor.com and igougo.com.

All this, of course, takes a long time – something you probably
don't have a lot of when you are busy planning the biggest day of
your life! HoneyMoney offer an excellent research service, where
they will do all the hard work and provide you with sample
itineraries of your chosen destination, with recommended hotels,

Get away!

activities and local tour operators. Then to top it all off, they'll do you a honeymoon wedding list so that all your friends then pay for the trip!

If you do decide to go it alone, don't leave too much to chance. You are likely to be exhausted after the wedding so, even if you are experienced backpackers, having at least your first few days accommodation, transfers, car hire and activities pre-booked will help reduce any stress and allow you to unwind and enjoy the rest of your holiday more.

A European jaunt

A honeymoon doesn't have to be far-flung and exotic, and our European neighbours have a lot to offer. With the average honeymoon costing in excess of £3,000, if you were to get a budget flight to Italy, just think of all the money you would have left over for extravagant accommodation and dining! And of course there are some world-renowned ski resorts in Europe – and what could be more romantic than cuddling up in front of a roaring fire after a day on the slopes? Provided you hold a EU passport you won't need any visas for any other EU countries, and you won't need to worry about inoculations or malaria tablets. With the growth of the budget airline industry you could save serious money on flights by opting to go to one of these routes – check out www.whichbudget.com to see which airlines fly where, and there are always good accommodation deals to be had on the Internet. You could also consider hiring your own villa, complete with swimming pool to guarantee you escape the crowds of holidaymakers.

Top Tip

Don't forget the travel insurance! It will give you added peace of mind that should anything go wrong, anything get stolen or either of you fall ill, you will be covered.

On the doorstep

Why even go abroad at all? With 781 islands, 68 castles, hundreds of miles of coastline, remote beaches, mountains, glens and countless golf courses in the Highlands alone, you could have a fantastic honeymoon right here in Bonnie Scotland. You won't need a passport or phrase book and there'll be no getting used to exchange rates and odd-looking bank notes! There is a vast array of accommodation, activities and places to visit so you needn't feel like you are staying at home. If you are travelling to Scotland to get married, then it would only make sense to stick around for the honeymoon and really get to know the country in which you tied the knot.

Your first stop for organising your Scottish honeymoon should be the VisitScotland website which has a huge amount of information for visitors with links to accommodation, activities and tour operators. They even have a subsection of the site dedicated to 'romantic Scotland'. Other useful websites are Travel Scotland and Rampant Scotland.

For the ultimate in luxury and a real once-in-a-lifetime experience, the five-star Royal Scotsman Train accommodates a maximum of 36 guests and offers one to seven night itineraries, with activities which include evening ceilidhs, guided walks, whisky distillery tours and golf. Or you could take to the seas aboard a tall ship. Highland Voyages offer a range of one to seven night itineraries, some of which include whale and dolphin watching. For the more active, Wilderness Scotland are just one company who can put together an exciting tailor made tour for you.

Timing is everything!

When should you go? Traditionally you should jet off the day after your wedding. However, if you are planning to be the last to leave your reception, you may appreciate a day to recover in a nice hotel at home before facing that long haul flight! Or, if you have your heart set on a particular destination, you may decide to postpone

Get away!

the honeymoon so as to avoid a monsoon season or uncomfortably high temperatures. Whatever you decide, if you are planning your honeymoon for a peak holiday season – book early! You don't want to be left disappointed that your first choice of resort is fully booked, and the later you leave it, the more expensive it is likely to get. If you do decide to postpone your honeymoon, check the conditions of any special honeymoon offers, as many are only valid for six months after the wedding.

On the ball!

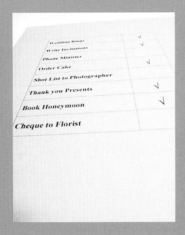

Being super-organised will help you to enjoy the process of planning your wedding even more. The more organised you are, the more time you will have on your hands to think about the finishing touches which will really make the difference to your big day.

July

Wed

Thu

Fri

August
S M T W T S
7 8 1 2 3 4 5
14 15 9 10 11 12
21 22 16 17 18 19
28 29 23 24 25 26 27
30 31

1

2

Sat

8

9

THE
BIG DAY!

16

The bridal countdown

It is a good idea to get as much organised as soon as possible – below is a guide, but if you can tick things off sooner, even better. You may find that you have a frenzy of organising and booking suppliers soon after you get engaged and then have several months without doing anything. This is fine because you can take your time and rest in the knowledge that you already have the major areas covered. Remember that popular venues, function bands, florists, photographers and caterers all get booked way in advance – sometimes years, so you will need to get moving quickly. Even if you haven't decided on details, you can book suppliers for the date just to ensure they will be available.

As soon as possible / 12 months before

Set a date
Establish your budget (include all parties who will be contributing)
Open a wedding account / credit card
Take out wedding insurance – you want to do this as soon as you start paying any deposits
Book a wedding consultant if you'll be using one
Work on the guest list to get a rough head count
Find and book a venue – for both ceremony and reception
Book a minister/registrar
Book a caterer
Book a band / DJ / musicians
Book a florist
Book a photographer and/or videographer
Choose your wedding party
Decide on your theme

Nine months before

Start looking for your dress
Start looking for the bridesmaids' dresses
Start thinking about readings and music
Book any entertainment you haven't already – casino, fireworks, magician, children's entertainer

On the ball!

Six months before

Finalise your order of service – including hymns, music and readings

Order the wedding invitations, orders of service, and any other wedding stationery you need

Order your wedding dress

Order your bridesmaids' dresses

Buy your shoes, lingerie and accessories

Book your hairdresser / make-up artist

Order your wedding cake

Start your beauty and exercise regime

Shop for groomsmen's outfits

Book your honeymoon

Four months before

Meet with caterer to discuss menus, wines and service style and organise a tasting

Have your first dress fitting

Start stocking up on candles, ribbons, table confetti and other accessories

Book all your beauty appointments for the week of the wedding – facial, make-up, hair, nails, tanning etc.

Choose where you will be holding your wedding list

Organise accommodation for your guests

Book transport for yourselves and your guests

Book your first night hotel

Order your favours, or decide what you are going go do if you are making them yourself

Two to three months before

Buy your wedding rings

Buy thank you gifts

Ensure passports and visas are up to date and check if you require any vaccinations for your honeymoon

Start shopping for your honeymoon wardrobe and accessories

Finalise the order of the day with the venue

Open your wedding list

Put together the inserts for your invitations – accommodation details etc.

Have tasting to finalise menu and wines

Four to eight weeks before

Mail invitations approximately eight weeks ahead of the wedding date

Submit marriage notice form and necessary documents to the registrar in the district in which the marriage will take place

Order foreign currency and/or travellers cheques for the honeymoon

Buy guest book

Do a first draft of the seating plan

Two to three weeks before

Have a hair and make-up run-through

Tweak your seating plan

Confirm details with the photographer, florist, etc.

Make a schedule of the day and hand it out to all your main suppliers and members of the wedding party

Advise caterer of final numbers

Have your final dress fitting – make sure you have all your lingerie, shoes and accessories

Collect your wedding rings

Ensure all your readers have a copy of their readings

Finish putting together favours, confetti bags, place cards etc.

Collect groom's and groomsmen's outfits

One week before

Place fees in envelopes to be given to the organist, minister, band etc.

Have a final facial, body scrub etc.

Get your engagement ring cleaned and polished so it is nice and sparkly for the big day

On the ball!

Pack for your honeymoon and wedding night

Put together your bride's emergency bag

Collect marriage schedule from the registrar (this will only be issued within seven days of the marriage)

Give a copy of the seating plan to the caterer/venue

Drop off any welcome packs/gifts at your guests' hotel

The day before

Go to the gym, take a long walk, or do some other stress-reducing activity

Have a manicure and pedicure

Double check your wedding outfit is all in place – and if possible at the venue where you will be getting ready

Drop off any items you can to the venue – ie. orders of service to the church, menus and name cards to the reception venue

Have a wedding rehearsal

Have a few drinks (but not too many!) with your close friends and family

Get a good night's sleep

Wash your hair as per your hairdresser's instructions (if you are having an up-do, they prefer your hair to be washed the day before, not the morning of the wedding)

Lists, lists, lists

Writing lists may well become an obsession of yours in the lead-up to your wedding! Use the above countdown to create your own master list of things to do. Add to this list everything you can think of that needs doing between now and your big day, no matter how large or small it is. Once you have done this, arrange it into an order of priority by months (and weeks and days as you get closer to the big day). This will make it seem more manageable than one long list, and having deadlines for each task will make it easier to tick them off. As you think of new things (and you will continually be thinking of new things, probably right up until the day before the wedding) slot them into an appropriate place on your list.

Break larger tasks down into smaller sections – for example, don't just put 'make favours'. Think of what exactly this entails and divide it up into smaller tasks – 'buy sweets', 'buy organza', 'buy ribbon', 'cut organza and ribbon sections' and 'make up favours', will allow you to spread the tasks over a period of time and tick things off as you go.

If you place an order for something from your list, don't just cross it off – make a note under the appropriate month of when it is due to arrive. That way, you will be reminded to chase it if it doesn't appear.

Managing your guest list

The easiest way to do this is to create a spreadsheet as follows:

Name	Invitation sent	Reply	Dietary requirements	Coach to ceremony	Coach from ceremony to reception	Coach to town	Gift received	Thank you card sent
Ceri Little	Yes	Yes	Vegetarian	Yes	Yes	Yes	Yes	Yes
Sarah & Paul Harding	Yes	Yes	None	No	No	Yes		
Vanessa & Sam Smith	Yes							
Phil Jones	Yes							
Sandy Roberts	Yes	Yes	Vegetarian	Yes	Yes	Yes	Yes	Yes
Claire & Barry Duncan	Yes							

Obviously you will need to change the headings to suit your own wedding, and you may need a different table for your evening guests. If you are organising hotel rooms, additional transport, or a champagne brunch the next day for example you should add this information in here too. Filling in this spreadsheet will ensure you have all the information in one place and can easily access the

On the ball!

information you require – just make everyone work off the same spreadsheet to save confusion.

Wedding file

A wedding file is a great idea for any bride. Your wedding file will enable you to keep all your bits and pieces together in one easy-to-find place, and will act as a great memento of your planning process. You should keep in it any pictures or articles you have cut out from magazines, business cards, useful web addresses or phone numbers, readings you like, and swatches of material and ribbon. It doesn't have to be an expensive purpose-made file, although these will tend to have all the useful sections you need – a countdown section, an address book section for your suppliers, budget planner, and a guest section where you can record their addresses, reply and gift details.

Top Tip

Carry a notebook with you in those last few weeks (or months) before your wedding. Things will pop into your head at the most inappropriate times – you'll suddenly remember on the bus to work that you haven't ordered a cake stand, or you'll be in a shop and hear a song you want to include on your playlist.

Wedding boxes

As soon as you start to buy things for your big day, get yourself two boxes and label them 'Ceremony' and 'Reception'. Make lists of all the things you will need to take with you and stick them on the boxes. You can then tick things off as they arrive and put them in the appropriate box. This way you will be able to see clearly what you already have and what you are still waiting for, and there should be no last minute running around, and nothing left behind! Example lists are shown below:

Ceremony

Orders of Service
Buttonholes/Corsages
Candles
Lighter/Matches
CDs
Confetti
Money to pay Minister/Registrar

Reception

Place cards
Menus
Table plans
Candles
Lighter/Matches
CDs
Napkin Rings/Ribbon
Favours
Thank you gifts
Table confetti
Disposable cameras

Detailed schedule

Below is an example of a detailed schedule of the big day. It will be helpful to create your own detailed schedule as it will firstly confirm that you haven't forgotten anything, and secondly will enable you to let everyone know quickly and easily where they should be and when. Start your schedule well in advance and add to it as things pop into your head.

Giving all your suppliers and members of the wedding party a copy of the entire written schedule will allow them to see where they fit in to the bigger picture. Your caterer, for example, may not realise the importance of setting up the tables by 11am and decide that they don't need to be set up until 1pm. If, however, they can see from the schedule that your florist is arriving at 11am to create the table centres, they will understand the importance of being punctual. Having everything written down in black and white will help ensure there are no misunderstandings.

Aim to give them a copy at least a week in advance so that if there are any queries or problems, they can be smoothed out well ahead of the big day. Remember to include contact names and phone numbers for all your suppliers, venue staff and main members of the wedding party on the schedule.

On the ball!

Time	Action
8:00 am	Caterers access to reception venue – commence set up of tables
9:00 am	Access to church Florist set up displays, best man drop off orders of service Groom drop overnight bags at hotel
10:00 am	Bride's hair appointment Buttonholes ready for collection – best man to collect
11:00 am	Caterers complete tables set up Friends 1 and 2 commence set up of table decorations
11:30 am	Florist deliver bouquets to bride's house
12:00 pm	Make-up artist to bride's house Photographer to bride's house for 'getting ready' shots Access for florist to reception venue – deliver and set up table centres
12:30 pm	Guests' coach arrives at hotel – usher 1 to count guests onto coach Formal photos at bride's house – including bridesmaids and family
1:00 pm	Ushers 2 and 3 arrive at church – light candles and reserve front two rows Organist arrives at church Coach leaves guests' hotel for church Car 3 collects groom and best man from groom's parents house
1:15 pm	Groom and best man arrive at church Cars 1 and 2 arrive at brides' house
1:30 pm	Guests' coach arrives at church – groom and best man to greet them Ushers 2 and 3 hand out orders of service and show guests to seats Cars 1 (bride and father) and 2 (bridesmaids and mother) depart for church
1:50 pm	Bridesmaids and bride's mother arrive at church

Groom and best man take places in church
Usher 1 to show mother of bride to seat

1:55 pm   Bride and father arrive at church
Piper commences piping

2:00 pm   **Ceremony commences**

2:30 pm   **Ceremony concludes**
Flower girl and bridesmaid 2 to hand out petal confetti at door
Photographs outside church – usher 1 to assist photographer with shot list

3:00 pm   Bride and groom depart for reception venue
Coaches depart for reception venue – usher 1 to ensure everyone on coach
Ushers 2 and 3 to move floral displays from church to reception venue

3:30 pm   Arrive at reception venue – usher 2 to show everyone to drinks reception
Jazz band commences
Bridal party to garden for photographs – usher 1 to assist photographer with shot list
Usher 3 to ensure bride and groom don't run out of drink!

4:45 pm   **Receiving line** – bride and groom only
Ushers 1 and 2 to move people toward receiving line
Usher 3 to ensure all guests can find their seats for dinner

5:15 pm   **Wedding breakfast commences**
Piper to pipe bride and groom into dining room – best man to ensure a dram of whisky available for piper
Bride and groom cut cake before sitting down

7:00 pm   **Speeches and toasts**
Best man to ensure bouquets for mothers in place

7:30 pm   **Evening guests arrive,** pay bar opens
Bride and groom greet evening guests
Chief bridesmaid ensure welcome drinks are ready for evening guests
Best man ensure band has arrived

8:00 pm   **First dance**

On the ball!

10:00 pm	**Evening buffet**
	Band break for half an hour – best man ensure CD ready
12:00 am	**Last dance**
	Coaches arrive – ushers to ensure everyone on correct coaches

Looking ahead

Changing your name

If you are going to change your name once you are married, you will need to let all or some of the following know:

Bank/Building Society
Club memberships
Credit companies (including store charge-card companies)
Doctor/Dentist
DVLA
Employer
Inland Revenue
Insurance companies
Investment companies
Loan companies
Local authority (council tax/electoral register)
Mobile phone company
Mortgage provider
Motoring organisations
Passport office
Pension companies
Professional institutes and bodies
School/College/University
Solicitor
TV licensing office
Utility companies – gas, electricity, water, phone and television providers

On the ball!

If you take your husband's surname after you marry, your marriage certificate is all the documentary evidence you require. Note that most companies require the original copy of your marriage certificate, so doing all this could take time. If you decide to have a double barrelled surname or have your maiden name as a middle name, a Deed Poll is usually required. See the website for more information: www.ukdps.co.uk

Anniversaries

Once it's all over – don't worry – there are still the anniversaries to look forward to! Below is a list of traditional wedding anniversaries:

1st	Paper	13th	Lace
2nd	Cotton	14th	Ivory
3rd	Leather	15th	Crystal
4th	Linen	20th	China
5th	Wood	25th	Silver
6th	Iron	30th	Pearl
7th	Wool	35th	Coral
8th	Bronze	40th	Ruby
9th	Pottery	45th	Sapphire
10th	Tin	50th	Gold
11th	Steel	55th	Emerald
12th	Silk	60th	Diamond

Showtime!

At last, the big day has actually arrived, and you finally get to enjoy what you have been planning for what seems like an eternity! So put on that fabulous dress, take a deep breath – and go enjoy the happiest day of your life!

Wedding day plan

It's not all about the planning – you actually get to go through with it too! Obviously the order of every wedding will differ, but below is an example of a wedding with a two o'clock ceremony in a church, with the reception held at a different venue.

8:00am   **Have a long luxurious shower**

You probably won't be able to sleep this morning through nerves and excitement and so will be up fairly early. Make the most of your time in the shower for last minute shaving, exfoliating and smothering yourself in your favourite body cream or spray. Remember to wear a top that buttons or zips up rather than needs to be pulled over your head as this could ruin your hair and make-up later.

9:00am   **Have a hearty breakfast with your family**

See if you can persuade someone to prepare a special breakfast while you are in the shower – American breakfast pancakes with maple syrup, smoked salmon and scrambled eggs or a good old fashioned fry-up. A glass of bucks fizz is always a good way to get the celebratory mood going at breakfast – just remember to pace yourself! Ensure you have something substantial – you may be too nervous to eat come lunchtime and you can be sure you will be having a few glasses of champagne before you sit down to your wedding meal.

10:00am   **Bride's hair appointment**

Remember to take your veil and tiara with you and to ask for plenty of hairspray. It may also be a good idea to have your mum or a bridesmaid with you so that the hairdresser can show them how to fix your hair if it drops.

Showtime!

11:00am   **Bride's make-up appointment**

Remember to ask your make-up artist for any tips in case you need to re-apply any of your makeup later. If you are doing your own make-up, be sure you give yourself plenty of time – your hands may not be as steady as normal and you may need to remove it and start again.

12 noon   **Start to get dressed in your wedding outfit**

Again, allow yourself plenty of time to fit your lingerie, dress, accessories etc. You can always sit and have a glass of bubbly and relax if you are ready early, but don't want to be panicking that you are running out of time and holding everything up.

12:30pm   **Photos of bride, bridesmaids and bride's family at home**

If you are having reportage photography, your photographer may have been with you for some time taking photos of you getting ready. For formal photographs the photographer will normally arrive slightly early to find suitable spots for your photos to be taken.

1:30pm   **Bride, father of the bride, bridesmaids and mother of the bride leave for church**

Guests begin arriving at church. Arrival music should be playing.

Groom greets guests at door of church and ushers show them to their seats.

1:45pm   **Groom and best man take their places at the front of the church**

1:55pm   **Bride arrives at the church.** Piper commences piping.

Mother of the bride is shown to her seat.

There may be a few additional photos of the bride outside the church.

Bride walks up the aisle on her father's arm and is followed by the bridesmaids.

2:00pm   **Ceremony commences**

2:30pm   **Ceremony concludes**

Bride and groom lead guests from the church. Formal photos are taken outside the church and confetti is thrown.

3:00pm   **Bride and groom leave for the reception venue**

Guests normally see the couple off and then make their own way to the reception venue afterwards.

3:30pm   **Drinks reception commences**

Some form of entertainment is normally provided and guests mingle whilst the formal photographs are taken. An usher should have been briefed to ensure that the right groups of people are available for the photographs when they are needed and that the bride and groom's champagne glasses are never empty!

4:45pm   **Receiving line**

Whoever is taking part in the receiving line welcome the guests to the wedding breakfast. The guest book is often set up at the receiving line, giving people something to do whilst they wait, and ensuring that everyone gets a chance to sign it. Be careful though, because if people take a long time to sign it, it could hold up the receiving line.

5:15pm   **Dinner is served!**

The bride and groom are announced and are piped into the banqueting room to the welcome of their guests. You may wish to cut the cake just before dinner, or later, either before or after the speeches.

7:00pm   **Toasts and speeches**

Showtime!

7:30pm   **Evening guests arrive**

The bride and groom should be at the door to welcome the new arrivals.

8:00pm   **First dance**

Obviously the timing of this depends on how much time is needed to turn the room around for the party and how much time your band or DJ requires to set up. The first dance is followed by dancing for the evening.

10:00pm   **Evening buffet served**

The evening buffet normally coincides with a break in the entertainment, especially if you are having a band. You should still have some kind of music for those who want to continue dancing. This is also a good time to throw the bouquet.

12 midnight **Last dance**

Depending on your venue, the last dance is either followed by coaches home, or is the sign for all guests to make their way to the residents' bar of the hotel to continue partying 'til the wee hours!

The bride's emergency bag

This should be given to a bridesmaid or your mother to look after throughout the day.

Make-up – lipstick, highlighter, cover-up, powder
Spare tights/stockings
Clear nail polish (for holes in stockings)
Hair clips
Tissues
Safety pins
Mini sewing kit
Money
Mobile phone

List of emergency phone numbers (florist, minister, piper, band)
Nail file
Painkillers
Blister plasters
Tampons

Bride's overnight bag

These are the things you will need with you at the venue where you get ready and also where you will spend the night. They are in addition to everything in the bride's emergency bag. Start packing this well in advance, and have a list which you can tick off clearly so that you can see what you have packed and what you still need to pack... don't leave it until the night before!

Wedding dress
Wedding shoes
Accessories – tiara, veil, hair accessories, jewellery, watch
Wedding lingerie, including tights or stockings
Make-up bag
Hairbrush, hair spray, hair dryer, hair straighteners or curlers
Toiletries – shampoo, conditioner, shower gel, razor, shaving gel, etc
Cleanser, toner, moisturiser
Toothbrush and toothpaste
Contact lens solution and spare lenses
Cotton wool pads and cotton buds
Tweezers
Manicure set and polish
Clothes for the next day, don't forget socks
Spare underwear – something sexy will do!
Shoes for the next day
Mobile phone and charger
Contraception

When things go wrong

A word of warning – everything may not go exactly to plan!
All you can do is to ensure you are as organised as you possibly can

Showtime!

be in the lead up to your big day and then RELAX AND ENJOY IT!
When things do go wrong, the best thing you can do is smile, take a
deep breath, and calmly think about what you can do to rectify it.
Panicking never gets anyone anywhere – it only makes things worse.
Crying doesn't do anyone any good – it will just upset everybody
else and leave you with a memory of you crying on your wedding
day.

Easier said than done, I know, but you have to try and make good
out of any potentially bad situation:

*'There was a power cut right when the band was about to start,
which lasted over an hour. I was devastated, but we ended up
having our first dance by candlelight, to an acoustic guitar and
the guests sang along – it was so romantic, and remains my
fondest memory of the whole day!'*

Susannah

If there is something you are worried about in the lead-up to your
wedding day – don't waste time worrying, make contingencies.
If you are worried about rain ruining the drinks reception on the
lawn, arrange for an alternative venue as a backup and get hold of
as many umbrellas as you can. If you are worried about a power
cut, hire a backup generator. Check with your suppliers what their
contingency plans are also – if you book a band through an agency
for example, it will normally be in their contract that they will find
a replacement in case of illness or other emergency. And of course,
invest in the all important wedding insurance.

Some things will be out of your hands – there's nothing you can do,
so stop worrying! If it happens, it happens. Try and make a joke
out of the situation if you are able, people will admire you a lot
more, and you want everyone to remember you as a happy bride
after all! What's the worst that could happen? The car doesn't turn
up? So you arrive a little late, in a taxi. The cake gets damaged?
So you hide the damage with some flowers from the garden, or

skip the cake cutting photographs and just serve slices with coffee –
most people won't even notice. If something worse does go wrong,
keep a level head and turn to your close friends and family for help
– they will probably be able to think a bit straighter than you.
And remember, that for every one thing that goes wrong, there's a
hundred that turned out perfectly… focus on them.

If I were to give only one piece of advice to brides-to-be, it
would be this: Enjoy your day as much as you can. You have
been planning every detail of this day for so long and it will pass
by so quickly – RELAX, SAVOUR EVERY MOMENT, AND HAVE FUN!

Your Scottish Wedding Directory

The directory has been divided into chapter sections.
The geographical location of Scottish companies, together
with phone numbers and, where appropriate, web
addresses are provided. As it's the digital age,
you needn't restrict your shopping to your local area,
or even to Scotland, so some useful addresses on
the web are also included where you can shop online to
your heart's content! Even if you never buy anything from
them, some of them are worth a look for inspiration.

First things first!

General wedding directories
www.scottishweddingdirectory.co.uk
www.thebestscottishweddings.co.uk
www.gretnaweddings.com
www.gretna-weddings.co.uk
www.wedsitescotland.com
romantic.visitscotland.com
www.confetti.co.uk
www.hitched.co.uk
www.loveweddings.co.uk
www.wedding-surf.co.uk

Wedding insurance
www.confetti.co.uk
www.eandl.co.uk
www.weddinginsurance.co.uk

Making it legal

General Register for Scotland
0131 314 4447
www.gro-scotland.gov.uk

The Church of Scotland
0131 225 5722
www.churchofscotland.org.uk

The Catholic Church
0131 452 8244
www.catholic-church.org.uk

Scottish Christian
www.scottishchristian.com (links to various churches and societies)

Location! Location! Location!

Historic Scotland
0131 668 8686
www.historic-scotland.gov.uk

National Trust for Scotland
www.nts.org.uk
www.scotlandbymail.com/functions

On the web
romantic.visitscotland.com
www.scottishweddingdirectory.com

www.castles.org/chatelaine
www.celticcastles.com
www.rampantscotland.com/castles.htm
www.weddingvenues.com

Marquee hire

Field & Lawn
Broxburn 01506 857938
Renfrew 0141 812 7787
www.fieldandlawn.com

Greenfield Marquees
Edinburgh 0131 558 8553
www.greenfieldmarquees.com

North of Scotland Marquees
Nairn 01667 455116
www.northofscotlandmarquees.com

I do!

Readings
www.biblegateway.com
www.bible-reading.com
www.hitched.co.uk
www.poetry.com
www.weddingguide.co.uk

Who wears what and how

Bridal Chain Stores

Berkertex Bride
Aberdeen 01224 651380
Edinburgh 0131 225 6646
Glasgow 0141 353 6262
www.bbride.com

Eleganza Spoza
Edinburgh 0131 524 7721
Glasgow 0141 248 3200
Hamilton 01698 303050
www.eleganza.co.uk

Pronuptia
Aberdeen 01224 632222
Edinburgh 0131 556 5018
Glasgow 0141 552 6736
www.pronuptia.co.uk

Boutiques

A Bridal Dream
Carnoustie 01241 410343
www.abridaldream.co.uk

Alma Ogilvie
Edinburgh 0131 220 5363
www.almaogilvie.co.uk

Altar Images
Bridge of Allan 01786 832298
www.wedding-gown.co.uk

Anne Priscilla Bridal
Glasgow 0141 222 2504
www.annepriscillabridal.co.uk

Ayrshire Bridal Centre
Ayr 01292 289901
www.ayrshire-bridal-centre.co.uk

Brides Delight
Aberdeen 01224 625999
www.bridesdelight.co.uk

Brides & Co.
Forres 01309 674444
www.bridesandco.co.uk

By Storm
Glasgow 0141 942 8900
www.bystorm.co.uk

Chantilly Bridal Fashion
Lossiemouth 01343 812448
www.chantillybride.com

Cuco Couture
Troon 01292 312112
www.cucocouture-bridalwear.co.uk

Diane Honeyman
Ayr 01292 282965
www.dianehoneyman.com

Emma Roy
Edinburgh 0131 557 2875

Enchante
Kirkcaldy 01592 263222
www.enchantebridal.co.uk

Exclusively Bridal
Inverness 01463 718171
www.exclusivelybridal.com

Infinity Bridal Couture
Dunfermline 01383 623490
www.infinitybridal.com

June Brides
Glasgow 0141 429 4162
www.junebrides.co.uk

Our Day Wedding Shop
Aberdeen 01224 715435
www.ourday.uk.com

Rachel Scott Bridal Couture
Edinburgh 0131 229 9775
www.rachelscottcouture.co.uk

Scottish Brides
Carnoustie 01241 855750
www.sol.co.uk/s/scotbrides

The Bridal Company
Glasgow 0141 637 4447
www.thebridalcompany.co.uk

Once-worn bridal boutiques

Patricia Rose Bridal Studio
Edinburgh 0131 226 5914

Dress Designers

Anne Matheson
Glasgow 0141 882 2791
www.annemathesonexclusivebridal
wear.co.uk

Clare Beechey Couture
Stirling 01259 769992
www.clarebeecheycouture.com

La Novia
Kinross 01577 865891
www.lanovia.co.uk

Liliana Dabic
Edinburgh 0131 466 7272
www.lilianadabic.com

Lindsay Fleming
Abington 01864 502 347
www.lindsayfleming.com
(Celtic/Medieval)

Lorraine Weselby
Edinburgh 0131 556 0038
www.weselby.co.uk

Opus Couture
West Kilbride 01294 824 838
www.opuscouture.com

On the web

www.allisonblake.com
www.amandawyatt.com
www.augustajones.com
www.hollywooddreams.co.uk
www.ianstuart-bride.com
www.maggiesotterobridal.com
www.morilee.com
www.pronovias.com
www.ritvawestenius.com
www.suzanneneville.com
www.designer-bridalwear.com

Shoes

Arabesque
Perth 01738 630574
www.arabesquedirect.co.uk

Carina Shoes
Edinburgh 0131 558 3344

Carol Currie
Glasgow 0141 248 7657

Dye for You/Zzag
Edinburgh 0131 557 3873
www.dye-for-you.co.uk

Uptown Girl Shoes
Cowdenbeath 01383 515400

Westend Dance Boutique
Glasgow 0141 959 0922

On the web

www.rainbow-club.co.uk
www.weddingshoesdirect.co.uk
www.ginashoes.com
www.jimmychoo.com
www.theaccessoryboutique.com

Accessories
Lingerie

Dimensions
Fraserburgh 01346 517968

Essential Lingerie
Wishaw 01698 358597
www.essentiallingerie.co.uk

La Jolie Madame
Edinburgh 0131 447 6715
www.lajoliemadame.com

On the web

www.agentprovocateur.com
www.figleaves.com
www.maxcleavage.com
www.bravissimo.com
www.thelingeriestore.co.uk
www.upliftedlingerie.co.uk

Tiaras, veils and jewellery

Angel Tiaras
Kirkcaldy 01592 580 224
www.angeltiaras.com

Baba C
Glasgow 0141 636 6848
www.baba-c.com

Elements Eternal
Glasgow 0141 946 2960
www.elementseternal.co.uk

Eleanor Barron
Glasgow 07989 967006
www.headdress.co.uk

Kam Yip
Edinburgh/Glasgow 07876 351970
www.kamyip.com

Tiaramendous
Annan 01461 201694
www.tiaramendous.co.uk

On the web

www.annalewis.com
www.atiara4u.com
www.butterflyoccasions.co.uk
www.nicolamcareejewellery.co.uk
www.tiararama.co.uk
www.weddingdesignbyapril.co.uk

Bridesmaids (see also Bridal)

www.watters.com
www.jimhjelmoccasions.com
www.veromia.co.uk

Hats

Elegance
Perth 01783 630 415

Hats by Maggie
Aberdeen 01224 575050
www.hatsbymaggie.co.uk

Holly O'Hara
Glasgow 07880 903 803
www.hollyoharamillinery.com

The Mad Hatter
Milngavie 0141 956 3146

Yvette Jelfs
Edinburgh 0131 225 696
www.yvettejelfs.com

Kilt hire

Geoffrey (Tailor)
Edinburgh 0131 557 0256
Glasgow 0141 331 2388
Oban 01631 570557
www.geoffreykilts.co.uk

McCalls
Aberdeen 01224 405300
Broughty Ferry 01382 730836
Edinburgh 0131 557 3979
Elgin 01343 540590
www.mccallsltd.com

Do it your way

Stationery

www.bellybuttondesigns.com
www.diddygilly.co.uk
www.itsourspecialday.com
www.funkyfairies.co.uk
www.ladybugcreations.co.uk
www.medievalscribe.co.uk
www.minniemoo.org.uk
www.whole-caboodle.co.uk

Make your own stationery:

www.madaboutcards.com
www.hobbycraft.co.uk
www.pdacardandcraft.co.uk
www.craftcreations.co.uk

Flowers

Acanthus
Roslin 0131 440 4649

Eden Creative Florists
Aberdeen 01224 636644
www.edenflowers.biz

Fiona Halliburton
Edinburgh 0131 317 9955
www.flowersbyfionahalliburton.co.uk

Florette
Paisley 0141 887 5679
www.florette.co.uk

Gretna Green Wedding Flowers
Gretna 01228 536096

Kirstie's Flowers
Troon 01292 316172
www.kirstiesflowers.com

Lilium
Edinburgh 0131 226 4999
www.lilium-florist.co.uk

Mood Flowers
Glasgow 0141 339 8820
www.moodflowers.com

Native Flowers
Glasgow 0141 341 0101
www.nativeflowers.co.uk

Ruby Flowers
Glasgow 0141 334 8666
www.rubyflowers.co.uk

Secret Garden
Edinburgh 0131 667 6662
www.secretgardenfloraldesign.co.uk

Simply Flowers
Aberdeen 01224 626 400
www.simplyflowers.org.uk

Stems
Edinburgh 0131 228 5575

Stephen Seedhouse
Nairn 01667 456223

On the web
www.flowers.org.uk
www.scottish-florists-online.co.uk

Cake

Au Gourmand
Edinburgh 0131 624 4666

Breezycakes
Haddington 01620 829555
www.breezycakes.co.uk

Cake Girl
Edinburgh 0131 229 1118

Cakes by Jacqueline
Dunfermline 01383 738 719
www.cakesbyjacqueline.co.uk

Classic Touch
Wishaw 01698 357700

Jenny's Cakes
Crossford 01555 860755
www.jennys-cakes.com

Patricia Macgowan
Stirling 01786 464 652
www.art2eat.co.uk

Plaisir du Chocolat
Edinburgh 0131 556 9524

Rainbow Sugarcraft
Peebles 01896 833 458
www.rainbowsugarcraft.co.uk

Sugar and Spice
Troon 01292 316830
www.sugarandspicetroon.com

The Cake and Chocolate Shop
Edinburgh 0131 228 4350
www.cakeandchocolateshop.co.uk

Too Good to Eat
Dalkeith 0131 663 2765
www.toogoodtoeat.co.uk

On the web
www.littlecakes.co.uk

Favours

Black Noir (decorative glass)
Grangemouth 07974 934336
www.black-noir.co.uk

Hebridean Toffee Company
Isle of Barra 01871 810 898
www.hebrideantoffeecompany.com

Highland Soaps
Spean Bridge 01397 712999
www.highlandsoaps.com

Just a Glass
Kirkcaldy 01592 653426
www.justaglass.co.uk

Kshocolat
Glasgow 0141 445 0077
Edinburgh 0131 555 7154
www.kshocolat.com

TB Watson (drinks gifts)
Dumfries 01387 256601
www.tbwatson.co.uk

Tobermory Handmade Chocolate
Argyll 01688 302526
www.tobermorychocolate.co.uk

Wineglass Jewellery
Glagow 0141 570 1531
www.wine-glass-jewellery.co.uk

On the web
www.aquarterof.com
www.butterflyoccasions.co.uk
www.chocoletta.com
www.forevermemories.co.uk
www.lovehearts.com
www.sweetthoughts.co.uk
www.theverynicecompany.com
www.unravelagift.com
www.villagesweetshop.com

Wedding crackers
www.nuptialnets.co.uk
www.totallycrackers.co.uk
www.weddingcracker.com

Candles
www.candlesontheweb.co.uk
www.onestopcandleshop.co.uk
www.waxandwane.co.uk

Confetti
www.confettidirect.co.uk
(real petals)
www.confoti.com (personalised
photo confetti)
www.petalpot.co.uk (real petals)

Ice sculptures
Highland Ice
Laurencekirk 01561 377 995

On the web
www.icesculpture.net
www.icesculpture.co.uk

Linen hire
88 Events
Glasgow 0141 445 2288
www.88eventscompany.com

PMG Events
Coatbridge 01236 434535
www.pmgevents.com

On the web
www.hss.com

Party accessories
www.partybox.co.uk
www.partypacks.co.uk
www.talkingtables.co.uk

Lighting companies
Fisher Productions
Edinburgh 0131 661 8880
Techniche
Edinburgh 07974156572
Tower Productions
Edinburgh 0131 552 0100

Picture Perfect
Photographers

Alex Coutts Photography
Dundee 01382 730761
www.acouttsphoto.com

Burnside Studios
Glasgow 0141 634 4765
www.burnsidestudios.co.uk

Ewen Forsyth
Lauder 01578 722411
www.ewenforsyth.co.uk

Gordon McGowan
Alexandria 01389 750773
www.gordonmcgowan.co.uk

Images of Morningside
Edinburgh 0131 452 9770
www.imagesofmorningside.com

James D Farrar Photography
Edinburgh 0131 557 6658
www.jamesfarrar.co.uk

Julie Lamont
Bothwell 01698 854968
www.julielamont.co.uk

Klaklak
Edinburgh 0131 623 9414
www.klaklak.com

Parris Photography
Hawick 01450 370523
www.parrisphotography.co.uk

Portraits Direct
Dundee 01382 543149
www.portraitsdirect.co.uk

Sarah Elizabeth Photography
Edinburgh 0131 448 0111
www.sarahelizabeth.co.uk

Silver Photography
Bishopton 01505 358967
www.silverphotography.co.uk

On the web

British Institute of Professional Photography
www.bipp.com

Guild of Wedding Photographers
www.gwp-uk.co.uk

Society of Wedding & Portrait Photographers
www.swpp.co.uk

Master Photographers Association
www.mpauk.com

Videographers

Design Scotland Video
Edinburgh 0845 226 2167
www.designscotland.net

Eclipse Video
Irvine 01294 217382
www.eclipsevideo.co.uk

Fairytale Productions
Glasgow 0141 339 1797
www.fairytaleproductions.co.uk

The-Video-Company.co.uk
Livingston 0808 108 096
www.the-video-company.co.uk

On the web

Association of Professional Video Makers
www.apv.org.uk

Institute of Videography
www.iov.co.uk

Get me to the church on time

Car hire

Caledonian Classics
Dollar 01259 742476
www.caledonianclassics.co.uk

Guy Salmon
Edinburgh 0131 347 8793
www.guysalmon.co.uk

Carriages

Caledon Carriages
Pathhead 01875 320825

Carriages
Cardrona 01896 830124

Clippity Clop Carriages
Canonbie 01461 800362

McIndoe
Falkirk 01324 861112

Chauffeur hire

Airdrie Wedding & Chauffeur Services
Airdrie 01236 763843
www.weddingandchauffeur
services.co.uk (carriages also)

Aisle Wedding Hire
Glasgow 0141 357 600

Chauffeured Limousines
Dalkeith 0131 447 7733
www.chauffeuredlimousines.co.uk

Collumbine Limousines
Falkirk 01324 831366
www.collumbine.com

Gretna Wedding Cars
Gretna 01461 338 291
www.gretnaweddingcars.co.uk

Harlequin Cars & Coaches
Dunblane 01786 822 547
www.harlequincoachesdunblane.
co.uk

Highland Beauford Wedding Car
Inverness 01463 831771
www.highland-wedding-car.co.uk

Limo Link USA
Dundee 01382 521 432
www.limolinkusa.co.uk

Ocean Wheels
Dalgety Bay 01383 825825
www.oceanwheels.co.uk

Platinum Limo Company
Edinburgh 0870 774 0880
www.theplatinumlimocompany.com

Stretched Out Limos
Edinburgh 0131 538 3999
www.stretchedoutlimos.co.uk

Waterside Classics Ltd
Glasgow 0141 647 0333
www.watersideweddings.com

Eat, drink and be merry

Caterers

Edinburgh Catering
Edinburgh 0131 558 9077
www.edinburghcatering.com

En Croute
Glasgow 0141 440 0114
www.encroute.co.uk

Grooms Catering
Glasgow 0141 639 4786
www.groomscatering.co.uk

Jaques & Lawrence
Haddington 01620 829 829
www.jlcatering.co.uk

Kensingtons
Glasgow 0141 333 0492
www.kensingtons-catering.co.uk

St Andrews Catering
St Andrews 01334 473 199
www.standrewscatering.com

The Creative Caterers
Perth 07745 429 060
www.thecreativecaterers.com

The Perfect Palate
Edinburgh 0131 553 4666
www.theperfectpalate.co.uk

Wilde Thyme
Crieff 01764 679736
www.wilde-thyme.co.uk

Wine merchants

Aitken's Wine Cellar
Dundee 01382 641 111
www.aitkenwines.com

Alliance Wine
Beith 01505 506060
www.alliancewine.co.uk

Cockburns of Leith
Edinburgh 0131 661 8400
www.winelist.co.uk

The Great Grog Company
Edinburgh 0131 662 4777
www.greatgrog.co.uk

Drinkon.com
St Andrews 01334 477333
www.drinkon.com

Raeburn Fine Wines
Edinburgh 0131 343 1159
www.raeburnfinewines.com

On the web

www.oddbins.com
www.majestic.co.uk
www.virginwines.com
www.laithwaites.co.uk

Chocolate fountains

Chocolate Falls
Port Seton 0808 118 1885
www.chocolatefalls-scotland.co.uk

Chocolate Fountain Scotland
Peebles 01896 833458
www.chocolatefountainscotland.co.uk

Chocolate Springs
Kilmarnock 01563 537788
www.chocolatesprings.co.uk

Coco Flow
Oban 01631 570555
www.cocoflow.co.uk

Entertainment agencies

Green Horn Agency
Dunfermline 01738 813 082
www.greenhornagency.co.uk

Hireaband.co.uk
01294 470820
www.hireaband.co.uk

Piping Services
Glasgow 0141 571 3877
www.pipingservices.com

Scotbase Entertainments
Paisley 0141 849 0333
www.scotbase.com

The Clann
East Kilbride 01355 241048
www.the-clann.co.uk

The Magic Agency
Glasgow 0141 577 6604
www.themagicagency.com

Fireworks

Scottish Fireworks & Displays
01592 872232
www.scottishfireworks.pwp.blue
yonder.co.uk

Stratus Fireworks
Inverness 01456 486729

Hey, good looking!

Hairdressers

Charlie Miller
Edinburgh 0131 225 1141
www.charliemiller.co.uk

Charlie Taylor
Dundee 01382 909090
Perth 01738 633221
St Andrews 01334 477770
www.charlie-taylor.co.uk

Cheynes
Edinburgh 0131 220 0777
www.cheyneshairdressing.com

Rainbow Room International
Ayr 01292 272450
Glasgow 0141 248 5300
Stirling 01786 448 789
www.rainbowroominternational.com

Saks
Aberdeen 01224 212 020
Edinburgh 0131 556 1475

Glasgow 0141 248 7788
www.sakshairandbeauty.com

Hair/make-up artists

Alamode
Edinburgh 07941 458391
www.alamodemakeup.com

LG makeup
Edinburgh 0131 466 2054
www.lgmakeup.co.uk

Made-up
Edinburgh 07801 659 584
www.made-up.net

Ramilia Hair and Makeup
Glasgow 0141 248 6162
www.ramiliahairandmake-up.co.uk

Sisstars
Glasgow 01360 770 320
www.sisstars.com

Beauty salons/spas

Adrianna's Hair & Beauty Salon
Aberdeen 01224 210 188
www.adriannas.com

Chi Health & Beauty
Glasgow 0141 226 1513
www.ch-i.co.uk

Escape Health Club
Edinburgh 0131 622 3800
www.escapehealthclubs.co.uk

Jacquies Beauty Salon
Dumfries 01387 269077
www.jacquiesbeauty.co.uk

One
Edinburgh 0131 221 7777
www.one-spa.com

The Beauty Studio
Bishopriggs 0141 762 4834
www.thebeautystudio.com

Zen Lifestyle
Edinburgh 0131 477 3535
www.zen-lifestyle.com

It's a wrap!

www.honeymoney.co.uk
www.johnlewisgiftlist.com
www.thealternativeweddinglist.com
www.weddinglistscotland.com
www.wrapit.co.uk

Girls behaving badly!

Travel forum/advice/reviews

thorntree.lonelyplanet.com
www.tripadvisor.com
www.travelintelligence.com

Hen packages

www.lastnightoffreedom.com
www.chillisauce.co.uk
www.sassyevents.com
www.activitysuperstore.com

Budget flights

www.whichbudget.com
www.flights4less.co.uk

Cheap hotel rooms

www.laterooms.com
www.venere.com
www.hotels.com

Get Away!

www.audleytravel.co.uk
www.bridgeandwickers.com
www.caribtours.co.uk
www.expressionsholidays.co.uk
www.harlequinholidays.com
www.partnershiptravel.co.uk
www.itcclassics.co.uk
www.seasonsinstyle.co.uk
www.somak.co.uk
www.discovercruises.co.uk
www.criuseopinion.com
www.intrepidtravel.com
www.journeylatinamerica.co.uk
www.reefandrainforest.co.uk
www.adventuredirectory.com

Forums and reviews

thorntree.lonelyplanet.com
www.cntraveller.com
www.tripadvisor.com
www.travelintelligence.com
www.igougo.com
www.gonomad.com

Scotland

www.visitscotland.com
www.travelscotland.co.uk
www.rampantscotland.com
www.royalscotsman.com
www.highlandvoyages.co.uk
www.wildernessscotland.com
www.celticcastles.com

sarah elizabeth
photography

relaxed contemporary photography

0131 448 0111
www.sarahelizabeth.co.uk
award winning wedding photography

SOME OTHER BOOKS PUBLISHED BY LUATH PRESS

The Scottish Wedding Book
G W Lockhart
ISBN 1 84282 010 9 PB £12.99

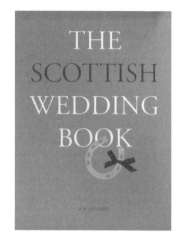

Scotland is the country of romance, with unique wedding traditions. Why get married anywhere else?

The Scottish Wedding Book is essential reading for all brides and grooms to be, and an ideal engagement present. Bridesmaids, best men and fathers of the bride may like to dip in too.

This book covers the traditions that make Scottish weddings so distinctive. It includes the technical and legal information necessary for a church or registry office ceremony, plus useful checklists, a Scots language version of the wedding service and locations of Scottish Kirks worldwide. Kilts, dresses, speeches, duties and dances; everything that makes a guid Scots shindig.

I'd call this a companion book; a learned little friend... covers everything from donning the kilt to dancing the night away.

THE HERALD

From seating arrangements to love poetry... essential reading for all brides and grooms looking for the undeniable romance of a tartan wedding.

DAILY RECORD

FICTION

Deadly Code
Lin Anderson
ISBN 1 905222 03 3 PB £9.99

The Burying Beetle
Ann Kelley
ISBN 1 905222 08 4 PB £6.99
ISBN 1 84282 099 0 PB £9.99

Selected Stories
Dilys Rose
ISBN 1 84282 077 X PB £7.99

Lord of Illusions
Dilys Rose
ISBN 1 84282 076 1 PB £7.99

Torch
Lin Anderson
ISBN 1 84282 042 7 PB £9.99

Heartland
John MacKay
ISBN 1 905222 11 4 PB £6.99

The Blue Moon Book
Anne MacLeod
ISBN 1 84282 061 3 PB £9.99

The Glasgow Dragon
Des Dillon
ISBN 1 84282 056 7 PB £9.99

Driftnet
Lin Anderson
ISBN 1 84282 034 6 PB £9.99

Milk Treading
Nick Smith
ISBN 1 84282 037 0 PB £6.99

The Kitty Killer Cult
Nick Smith
ISBN 1 84282 039 7 PB £9.99

The Road Dance
John MacKay
ISBN 1 84282 024 9 PB £6.99

**Outlandish Affairs:
An Anthology of Amorous
Encounters**
Edited and introduced by Evan
Rosenthal and Amanda Robinson
ISBN 1 84282 055 9 PB £9.99

POETRY

**Parallel Worlds: Poems in
Shetlandic and English [book]**
Christine De Luca
ISBN 1 905222 13 0 PB £8.99

Jane
Anita Govan
ISBN 1 905222 14 9 PB £6.99

**The Wallace Muse: Poems and
artworks inspired by the life
and legend of William Wallace**
compiled and edited by Lesley
Duncan and Elspeth King
ISBN 1 905222 29 7 PB £7.99

**Voyage of Intent: Sonnets and
essays from the Scottish
Parliament**
James Robertson
ISBN 1 905222 26 2 PB £6.99

**Tweed Rivers: New writing and
art inspired by the rivers of the
Tweed catchment**
edited by Ken Cockburn and
James Carter
ISBN 1 905222 25 4 PB £9.99

Poems to be Read Aloud
introduced by Tom Atkinson
ISBN 0 946487 00 6 PB £5.00

Scots Poems to be Read Aloud
introduced by Stuart McHardy
ISBN 0 946487 81 2 PB £5.00

SOME OTHER BOOKS PUBLISHED BY LUATH PRESS

The Whisky Muse:
Scotch whisky in poem & song
Robin Laing
ISBN 1 84282 041 9 PB £7.99

Into the Blue Wavelengths
Roderick Watson
ISBN 1 84282 075 3 PB £8.99

FOOD & DRINK

The Glasgow 100:
The independent guide to the
best places to eat
David Phillips
ISBN 1 84282 068 0 PB £4.99

First Foods Fast: How to
prepare good simple meals for
your baby
Lara Boyd
ISBN 1 84282 002 8 PB £4.99

Edinburgh and Leith Pub Guide
Stuart McHardy
ISBN 0 946487 80 4 PB £4.95

BIOGRAPHY

Willie Park Junior: The man who
took golf to the world
Walter Stephen
ISBN 1 905222 21 1 HB £25.00

Vet in the Country
Russell Lyon
ISBN 1 84282 067 2 PB £9.99

Not Nebuchadnezzar: In search
of identities
Jenni Calder
ISBN 1 84282 060 5 PB £9.99

Think Global, Act Local: The life
and legacy of Patrick Geddes
Edited by Walter Stephen
ISBN 1 84282 079 6 PB £12.99

The Last Lighthouse
Sharma Krauskopf
ISBN 0 946487 96 0 PB £7.99

Tobermory Teuchter
Peter Macnab
ISBN 0 946487 41 3 PB £7.99

Bare Feet & Tackety Boots
Archie Cameron
ISBN 0 946487 17 0 PB £7.95

SOCIAL HISTORY

This City Now: Glasgow and its
working class past
Ian R Mitchell
ISBN 1 84282 082 6 PB £12.99

HISTORY

Scotch on the Rocks: The true
story behind Whisky Galore
Arthur Swinson
ISBN 1 905222 09 2 PB £7.99

Braveheart: From Hollywood to
Holyrood
Lin Anderson
ISBN 1 84282 066 4 PB £7.99

Reportage Scotland: Scottish
history in the voices of those
who were there
Louise Yeoman
ISBN 1 84282 051 6 PB £7.99

POLITICS AND
CURRENT ISSUES

Global Scots: Voices from Afar
Kenny MacAskill and Henry McLeish
ISBN 1 905222 37 8 PB £9.99

Agenda for a New Scotland:
Visions of Scotland 2020
Edited by Kenny MacAskill
ISBN 1 905222 00 9 PB £9.99

Getting it Together: the Campaign for a Scottish Assembly/Parliament
Bob McLean
ISBN 1 905222 02 5 PB £12.99

Scotlands of the Mind
Angus Calder
ISBN 1 84282 008 7 PB £9.99

WALK WITH LUATH

50 Classic Routes on Scottish Mountains
Ralph Storer
ISBN 1 84282 091 5 PB £6.99

Skye 360: Walking the coast-line of Skye
Andrew Dempster
ISBN 0 946487 85 5 PB £8.99

The Joy of Hillwalking
Ralph Storer
ISBN 1 84282 069 9 PB £7.50

Scotland's Mountains before the Mountaineers
Ian R Mitchell
ISBN 0 946487 39 1 PB £9.99

Mountain Days & Bothy Nights
Dave Brown & Ian R Mitchell
ISBN 0 946487 15 4 PB £7.50

Of Big Hills and Wee Men
Peter Kemp
ISBN 1 84282 052 4 PB £7.99

FOLKLORE

Luath Storyteller: Highland Myths & Legends (new edition)
George W Macpherson
ISBN 1 84282 064 8 PB £5.99

Luath Storyteller: Tales of the Picts
Stuart McHardy
ISBN 1 84282 097 4 PB £5.99

Tales of the North Coast
Alan Temperley
ISBN 0 946487 18 9 PB £8.99

LANGUAGE

Luath Scots Language Learner [Book]
L Colin Wilson
ISBN 0 946487 91 X PB £9.99

Luath Scots Language Learner [Double Audio CD Set]
L Colin Wilson
ISBN 1 84282 026 5 CD £16.99

ISLANDS

Lewis and Harris: History and Pre-History
Francis Thompson
ISBN 0 946487 77 4 PB £5.99

The Islands that Roofed the World: Easdale, Belnahua, Luing & Seil
Mary Withall
ISBN 0 946487 76 6 PB £4.99

Rum: Nature's Island
Magnus Magnusson
ISBN 0 946487 32 4 PB £7.95

Luath Press Limited

committed to publishing well written books worth reading

LUATH PRESS takes its name from Robert Burns, whose little collie Luath (*Gael.*, swift or nimble) tripped up Jean Armour at a wedding and gave him the chance to speak to the woman who was to be his wife and the abiding love of his life. Burns called one of *The Twa Dogs* Luath after Cuchullin's hunting dog in *Ossian's Fingal*. Luath Press was established in 1981 in the heart of Burns country, and is now based a few steps up the road from Burns' first lodgings on Edinburgh's Royal Mile.

Luath offers you distinctive writing with a hint of unexpected pleasures.

Most bookshops in the UK, the US, Canada, Australia, New Zealand and parts of Europe either carry our books in stock or can order them for you. To order direct from us, please send a £sterling cheque, postal order, international money order or your credit card details (number, address of cardholder and expiry date) to us at the address below. Please add post and packing as follows: UK – £1.00 per delivery address; overseas surface mail – £2.50 per delivery address; overseas airmail – £3.50 for the first book to each delivery address, plus £1.00 for each additional book by airmail to the same address. If your order is a gift, we will happily enclose your card or message at no extra charge.

Luath Press Limited
543/2 Castlehill
The Royal Mile
Edinburgh EH1 2ND
Scotland
Telephone: 0131 225 4326 (24 hours)
Fax: 0131 225 4324
email: gavin.macdougall@luath.co.uk
Website: www.luath.co.uk